AROUND miami WITH KIDS

By Jen Karetnick

Fodor's Travel Publications
New York • Toronto • London • Sydney • Auckland

www.fodors.com

CREDITS

Writer: Jen Karetnick

Series Editors: Karen Cure, Caroline Haberfeld
Editor: William Travis
Editorial Production: Stacey Kulig
Production/Manufacturing: Robert Shields

Design: Fabrizio La Rocca, *creative director*;
Tigist Getachew, *art director*
Illustration and Series Design: Rico Lins, Keren Ora
Admoni/Rico Lins Studio

ABOUT THE WRITER

Jen Karetnick reviews restaurants for Miami *New Times* and
New Times Broward/Palm Beach, and is the author of *Miami
Restaurant Recipes* (Tierra Publications, 2000). A published
poet and freelance food-and-travel journalist, she
contributes to *Diversion, Poets & Writers,* and Fodor's *Miami*
and *Florida* books. She lives in Miami Shores with her
husband and two children.

First Edition
ISBN 0–679–00727–X
ISSN 1531–3387

Important Tip

Although all prices, opening times, and other details in this
book are based on information supplied to us at press time,
changes occur all the time in the travel world, and Fodor's
cannot accept responsibility for facts that become outdat-
ed or for inadvertent errors or omissions. So always confirm
information when it matters, especially if you're making a
detour to visit a specific place.

Special Sales

Fodor's Travel Publications are available at special
discounts for bulk purchases for sales promotions or
premiums. Special editions, including personalized covers,
excerpts of existing guides, and corporate imprints, can be
created in large quantities for special needs. For more
information, contact your local bookseller or Special
Markets, Fodor's Travel Publications, 280 Park Avenue, New
York, NY 10017. Inquiries from Canada should be directed
to your local Canadian bookseller or sent to Random House
of Canada, Ltd., Marketing Dept., 2775 Matheson Boulevard
East, Mississauga, Ontario L4W 4P7. Inquiries from the
United Kingdom should be sent to Fodor's Travel
Publications, 20 Vauxhall Bridge Road, London, England
SW1V 2SA.

PRINTED IN THE UNITED STATES OF AMERICA
10 9 8 7 6 5 4 3 2 1

CONTENTS

WELCOME TO GREAT DAYS!

B etween pick-ups, drop-offs, and after-school activities, organizing a family's schedule is one full-time job. Planning for some fun time together shouldn't be another. That's where this book helps out. In creating it, our parent-experts have done all the legwork, so you don't have to. Open to any page and you'll find a great day together already planned out. You can read about the main event, check our age-appropriateness ratings to make sure it's right for your family, pick up some smart tips, and find out where to grab a bite nearby.

HOW TO SAVE MONEY
Taking a whole family on an outing can be pricey, but there are ways to save.

1. Always ask about discounts at ticket booths. We list admission prices only for adults and kids, but an affiliation (and your ID) may get you a break. If you want to support a specific institution, consider buying a family membership up front. Usually these pay for themselves after a couple of visits, and sometimes they come with other good perks—gift-shop and parking discounts, and so on.

2. Keep an eyed peeled for coupons. They'll save you $2 or $3 a head and you can find them everywhere from the supermarket to your pediatrician's office. Combination tickets, sometimes offered by groups of attractions, cost less than if you pay each admission individually.

3. Try to go on free days. Some attractions let you in at no charge on day a month or one day a week after a certain time.

GOOD TIMING

Most attractions with kid appeal are busy when school is out. Field-trip destinations are sometimes swamped on school days, but these groups tend to leave by early afternoon, so weekdays after 2 during the school year can be an excellent time to visit museums, zoos, and aquariums. Outdoors, consider going after a rain—there's nothing like a downpour to clear away crowds. If you go on a holiday, call ahead—we list only the usual operating hours.

SAFETY CATCH

Take a few sensible precautions. Show your kids how to recognize staff or security people when you arrive. And designate a meeting time and place—some visible landmark—in case you become separated. It goes without saying that you should keep a close eye on your children at all times, especially if they are small.

FINAL THOUGHTS

One more pointer: If your kids have specific interests, ask about behind-the-scenes tours at places such as newspapers, public utilities, TV stations, and even airports. (Though many tours are primarily for school groups, a family can often be accommodated as well.) Finally, we'd love to hear yours: What did you and your kids think about the places we recommend? Have you found other places we should include? Send us your ideas via e-mail (c/o editors@fodors.com, specifying the name of this book on the subject line) or snail mail (c/o Around Miami with Kids, Fodor's Travel Publications, 280 Park Avenue, New York, NY 10017). In the meantime, have a great day around Miami with your kids.

THE EDITORS

ACTORS' PLAYHOUSE AT THE
MIRACLE THEATRE

T he Actors' Playhouse is dedicated to entertaining and culturally enriching audiences by producing quality live theater. Its ensemble of actors, directors, designers, and visual artists bring new life to classic stories, enchanting both children and adults.

The somewhat tongue-in-cheek shows are usually based on fairy tales, and in the past, the Actors' Playhouse has performed such gems as *The Stone-Age Cinderella, The Emperor's New Clothes,* and *The Princess and the Pea.* Expect some humorous liberties to be taken with the traditional scripts, all in the name of contemporary culture. The shows last about one hour and are preceded by a short lecture on theater etiquette and post-scripted by a 15-minute question-and-answer session with one or more of the actors.

The Actors' Playhouse relocated to the Miracle Theatre from a mall in Kendall in the early '90s. It was a good move—the theater itself is an art deco gem, a renovated, 600-seat

HEY, KIDS! Remember to be courteous when watching a performance. Eating popcorn or candy, walking around, or talking will distract the actors. It's best to stay in your seat until the house lights come up, signaling intermission or the end of the play. Then you can talk, laugh, and move around again.

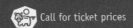 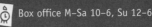

280 Miracle Mile, Coral Gables

Call for ticket prices

Box office M-Sa 10-6, Su 12-6

305/444-9293

2 and up

hall with plush, crushed velvet chairs. This theater has two parts: the proscenium stage, where productions such as Steve Martin's *Picasso at the Lapin Agile* are staged, and the Children's Balcony Theater, where the professional Equity troupe, the Actors' Playhouse, puts on matinees for the kids. Children over the age of 12 may even be able to appreciate some of the major productions, particularly the Andrew Lloyd Webber musicals *Jesus Christ Superstar* and *Joseph and the Amazing Technicolor Dreamcoat*. For performance listings, see the *Miami Herald* weekend section.

For children and teens who want to experience a theater production firsthand, one-act workshops are offered during the spring, summer, and fall. Call for more details.

KEEP IN MIND
Parking can be tight on Miracle Mile, but there are plenty of metered spaces and municipal lots in the neighborhood. Make sure to bring enough change with you. Coral Gables police are fairly vigilant about giving out parking tickets, which can really add to the cost of your outing.

KID-FRIENDLY EATS Stroll across the street for a hamburger at **John Martin's** (253 Miracle Mile, tel. 305/445–3777), a busy, family-friendly Irish pub. Or take a seat at **Biscayne Miracle Mile Cafeteria** (147 Miracle Mile, tel. 305/444–9005), a self-serve joint that offers plenty of home-style Southern favorites such as fried chicken and mashed potatoes with gravy.

A.D. BARNES PARK AND SENSE OF
WONDER NATURE CENTER

Children love A.D. Barnes for the Sense of Wonder Nature Center and Trail, an interactive, hands-on adventure made up of outdoor exhibits. The idea helps children learn to appreciate nature by using different senses.

Here, kids can touch and smell the dried palm fronds, from which Seminole and Miccosukee Indians make chickees, or the open-air huts in which they live. At the pond, they can listen to a waterfall splashing and watch fish and turtles being fed. A third section of the trail allows them to smell the differences between rosemary and basil in an herb garden.

As Miami's parks go, this one's relatively small, only about 62 acres. But as you'll soon find out, the park distinguishes itself in several areas. Most important, the park has been designed for kids with disabilities, from those in wheelchairs to those suffering from asthma.

KID-FRIENDLY EATS Toward South Miami, along S.W. 72nd Street, stop at **Deli Lane Cafe** (7230 S.W. 59th Ave., tel. 305/665–0606) for a sandwich or **Koo Koo Roo** (5850 S.W. 72nd St., tel. 305/661–1933) for healthy, fast-food chicken.

KEEP IN MIND A.D. Barnes Park publishes *Tropical Trails Magazine*, a terrific guide to ecologic and environmental goings-on in South Florida. The magazine contains articles on native wildlife, nature photography, detailed line drawings, recipes, and a children's section complete with cartoons. The calendar listing of upcoming nature walks and tours is especially handy.

3401 S.W. 72nd Ave., South Miami

 Free; pool extra

Daily 8–sunset

All ages

 305/662-4124

Apart from the paved, wheelchair-friendly paths, the park also supplies a wheelchair-accessible tree house—actually a 200-ft ramp that extends 12 ft above the ground into a cluster of trees. (The tree house is great for strollers, too.) In addition, a solar-heated swimming pool has a hydraulic floor, which can be raised and lowered to accommodate wheelchairs.

In various areas of the park, you can go for a run, bike on a path, or guard toddlers as they play in the "tot lot," a playground sized just for the wee folk. A freshwater lake stocked by the Parks Department with bass can provide a whole afternoon's diversion, depending on if the fish are biting or not. At the end of the day, everyone can cool off in the swimming pool or have a picnic.

HEY, KIDS! The five senses are sight, sound, taste, touch, and smell. If you're lucky, you get to use all five. But some kids aren't as lucky, and have lost the use of one or more senses. You can understand how those kids relate to the world around them by trying an experiment. Go on the nature walk with a partner. Blindfold yourself, or just keep your eyes closed, and ask your partner to guide you along the trail. Then see if you can identify all the exhibits simply by touching, smelling, or hearing them.

ADVENTURER'S COVE PLAY-GROUND

Given the subtropical climate of Miami, a rainy day is bound to happen. What's a family to do? Head for the malls is the most likely solution, but shopping can bore kids under 10, who'd much rather play outdoors. Aventura Mall not only has plenty of shopping and chain restaurants but also is home to Adventurer's Cove, the only indoor mall playground in Miami, which provides activities for restless babies, toddlers, and preschoolers—and plenty of people-watching for the older kids.

On the first floor of the mall in front of Sears, Adventurer's Cove has the little ones in mind. No one over the age of 8 or the height of 4 ft is allowed entrance, except for parents. Leave the strollers outside the fenced-in area and head to the jungle gym with a pirate's theme. Kids can't wait to get their hands on the captain's wheel or slide down the ultrawide slide into the "ocean." Scattered around the jungle gym, soft marine play sculptures shaped like leaping dolphins tempt climbers to clamber on up and ride 'em. Don't worry if the 3-year-old takes a tumble—the floor is padded.

KEEP IN MIND Parking can be tight at the newest end of the mall, particularly near the chain restaurants. Valet parking is also an option for those not wishing to make a potential long trek, especially with kids. After all, it'll take you nearly as long to find a spot as it will to wait for your car to be brought to the front afterward.

 Aventura Mall, 19501 Biscayne Blvd., Aventura

n/a

 Free

 Daily 10–9

8 and under

Adjacent to the playground, a small train takes youngsters for a choo-choo ride around a small sculpture park designed to reflect the current season. Buying several trips at a time ($1.50 per ride) is recommended so toddlers don't feel short-shrifted after a single go-round. If your visit to Miami coincides with Christmas or Easter, chances are you can purchase a keepsake photo of your youngster in the arms of Santa or the Easter Bunny.

The mall itself is large and completely enclosed, so a stroller is necessary if you decide to shop. Fortunately, if you've forgotten to bring a stroller along, you can rent one near Macy's.

KID-FRIENDLY EATS The mall has plenty of restaurants, but the most popular ones with kids are the **Cheesecake Factory** (tel. 305/792–9696), where portions are big enough to split, and the **Rainforest Café** (tel. 305/792–8001), where life-size mechanical elephants and alligators entertain children as they eat.

HEY, KIDS! In October 1908, Miami had its rainiest month ever, with an astonishing 28 inches. But Miami is no stranger to water. In fact, the Indian name "Miami" means "sweet water," which refers to the freshwater that funnels down from the Everglades to the Miami River.

AMELIA EARHART PARK

Options Unlimited is an accurate description for this 515-acre park, which was developed with every age group in mind. Whether your kids are swimmers, boaters, cyclists, joggers, pony riders, or just plain ol' jungle-gym climbers, they'll find suitable action—or suitable rest—in this preserve.

The highlight of the park is the Bill Graham Farm Village, a re-created Florida homestead. After entering the farm through a bougainvillea-laden trellis, the youngsters should immediately head for the barn's petting area. Kids will delight in feeding and stroking the numerous cows, horses, ponies, goats, chickens, pigs, sheep, geese, and even a donkey or two. You might cringe at the germs that can accumulate on the kids' hands, so be prepared for a little slobber and a lot of barnyard dirt. Have plenty of moist wipes handy.

After your kids have had their fill of petting, head over to the Demonstration Hall to watch homesteaders milk cows or toss horseshoes. Then, move on to Earhart Hall for

HEY, KIDS!
Bass like dark, quiet places in the water and usually rest in places where vegetation is heavy, like in patches of grass or under lily pads. Try to cast your line near those places for a nibble on your hook. The trick is making sure not to snag your line.

KEEP IN MIND
Brace yourself for cries of "I want a pony!" The animals here are particularly well kempt and well behaved, which may prompt a 4-year-old to think that a horse will make a good pet. One sure solution: Ask the trainers how much manure they have to shovel on a daily basis. Then tell your kids it'll be their job. Problem solved.

401 E. 65th St., Hialeah

 $3.50 per car

Daily 9–sunset

All ages

 305/769–2693

All ages

exhibits of early farm equipment—the scythe looks particularly menacing—and lectures on subjects such as home canning and organic gardening, which will interest kids of all ages. The Crop Area showcases acres of shiny, happy sunflowers, and a boiling shed behind it processes sugar into molasses. The Smokehouse is next in line, easily located by your nose and your kids' growling stomachs, where you can savor the flavor of smoked turkeys and hams. From here, kids can ride ponies, jump in a haystack, or sit atop an old-fashioned tractor.

Longing for more respite? Head down to the Fishing Rock, where your kids can try catching bass in the freshwater lake. Or set them free on the Tom Sawyer Play Island, a mecca for rock-climbing adventurers. The island can only be broached by suspension bridge, and is surrounded by water, so keep an eye on the youngest ones.

KID-FRIENDLY EATS The air-conditioned **General Store** (tel. 305/681–4011) is fully stocked with every sugar-lover's fantasy, including ice cream and lots of old-fashioned goodies. Picnic lunches are definite pluses if you plan on spending the day, unless you intend to catch your own from the Fishing Rock.

AMERICAN POLICE HALL OF FAME & MUSEUM

64

Upon first glance, the life-size police car crawling up the exterior wall makes this place look more like a police station than a police museum. Yet inside its walls, you will experience the historical journey of law enforcement through its rich collection of artifacts and educational displays. It's also the nation's only police museum that honors all officers who have served in federal, state, county, and local departments.

A massive 400-ton white marble display is your first stop. This moving memorial, dedicated to the memory of the men and women who have died in the line of duty, lists the names of American police officers killed since 1960. It can be a sobering experience, to say the least, so remind your children that respect and quiet is always necessary.

On the second floor, the museum proudly displays its collection of more than 10,000 police artifacts dating from the 1700s. No doubt preteens will be awed by the collections of

HEY, KIDS! Did you know that police dogs are considered police themselves? When killed in the line of duty, they are honored by the entire police force and given special funerals. You can read the names of these heroic animals engraved on the special monument dedicated to all the canines who have helped fight crime.

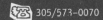
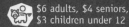
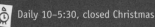
guns, radar units, uniforms, and badges. Edifying exhibits featuring courageous heroes and notorious criminals encourage hands-on participation. Kids can test their crime-solving skills at simulated crime scenes. Other, less innocent exhibits include a prison cell, a gas chamber, and an electric chair known as "Old Sparky" within the state of Florida.

An informative guided tour is recommended to help explain exhibits. Apart from serving as a memorial, the museum strives to educate the public about the nature of police work and provide monetary help and scholarships to the families of those who died in the field.

KID-FRIENDLY EATS Head north on Biscayne Boulevard, and you'll come to **Soyka** (5556 Biscayne Blvd., tel. 305/759-3117), a stylish bistro that likes kids so much it has homemade chocolate chip cookies on the children's menu. For a more ethnic experience, visit **Edelweiss** (2655 Biscayne Blvd., tel. 305/573-4421) for German bratwurst, schnitzel, and strudel.

KEEP IN MIND Some of the exhibits and displays may be too bold and gruesome for children. Even older kids might need some sort of discussion about these exhibits and displays for sense of closure. Before entering the museum, stop at the front desk for a brochure to determine which exhibits are appropriate for your children.

ANCIENT SPANISH MONASTERY

Ancient just about says it all. The Church of St. Bernard de Clairvaux was built in Sacramenia, in the Province of Segovia, Spain, and dates from AD 1141, a date that's sure to boggle minds. It survived wars, natural catastrophes, and other potential disasters for centuries—it was once even used as a granary and stables during the 1800s. So how did this ancient Spanish monastery wind up in Miami?

This question will briefly fascinate children, as will the answer. In 1925 millionaire spendthrift William Randolph Hearst purchased the place after touring it during a visit to Spain. He then had it dismantled, stone by stone, and shipped it to the United States, packed in hay. It turns out, however, that due to an outbreak of hoof-and-mouth disease onboard the ship, the boxes were confiscated, the possibly infected hay was burned, and the stones were quarantined. Hearst eventually lost interest, not to mention the funds necessary, to free and reconstruct the stones, so the monastery sat—in more bits and pieces than a Lego set—in a warehouse for 26 years.

KID-FRIENDLY EATS Got a yen for a meat loaf melt? Head just a little north and a little east to **Katz Deli** (3585 N.E. 207th St., tel. 305/936–9555) for delicacies of all kinds, including matzoh ball soup and stuffed cabbage.

HEY, KIDS! Hoof-and-mouth disease is a condition that affects cattle. You may have heard of something called hand-foot-mouth disease, or even had it yourself. Hand-foot-mouth disease is a mild condition that occurs in humans, causing blisters on the palms of the hands and soles of the feet. Although it sounds similar, it's not related to what the cows get.

16711 W. Dixie Hwy., North Miami Beach

 $4 adults, $2.50 seniors, $1 children under 12

M–Sa 10–4, Su 12–4, closed major holidays

305/945–1462

 All ages

In 1952 two Miami entrepreneurs, looking to construct an original tourist attraction, bought the monastery and shipped the pieces down to "Magic City," Miami's nickname. When the stones arrived, however, it was difficult to tell how the stones were supposed to be assembled. The new owners had to guess how to reconstruct the monastery, kind of like trying to complete a jigsaw puzzle without a picture to guide you. The end result, which took 19 months and $1.5 million to complete, is still a bit of a mystery to architects. Some of the unmatched stones never even made it into the building and were used instead to build the present parish hall and pave the courtyard.

Today, the monastery is an Episcopal church. Remind your children that respect and quiet are always necessary.

KEEP IN MIND Though the monastery and its gardens are quite pretty, kids will quickly get bored after the novelty of its history wears off. Keep them occupied by having them search for places that look like they weren't properly put together. Touring should only take about 30 minutes or so. Try to avoid visiting weekends because the grounds are frequently rented for weddings and other affairs.

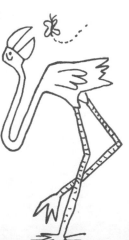

ARCH CREEK PARK AND MUSEUM

This small park is actually an archaeological dig site, presenting one of the more interesting activities in Miami. Families can participate in archaeological digs, held periodically throughout the year. The digs take about three hours, and a chance to discover some rare relic will thrill children of all ages. Younger children may not understand what's going on, but they'll have fun just getting down and dirty anyway.

The centerpiece of this park is the natural limestone bridge formation, once used by migrating Seminole Indians and their ancestors, the now-extinct Tequesta Indians. Historians have unearthed many artifacts—such as arrowheads, spear points, and pottery—from these native peoples, which are displayed in the homesteadlike museum. Whether or not your children will appreciate the history lesson, they'll certainly enjoy sorting through the dirt or hopping over the ancient bridge.

Volunteer naturalists give tours on Saturday morning, and the highlight of the tour is a visit to the wildlife sanctuary. Here, injured creatures are nurtured before being returned

HEY, KIDS! When something is "exotic," it means it's not native to an area. For example, iguanas are classified as exotic in Miami, since they weren't born into the wild here. An exotic plant is one that has been introduced to a region for a specific reason but then took root on its own.

 1855 N.E. 135 St., North Miami

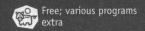 Free; various programs extra

 Daily 9–5

305/944-6111

 All ages

to the wild. You can stroll among the wildflowers along the nature trail, which is comfortably shaded by cypress, pines, and hardwood hammocks. The walk takes about 30 minutes, longer with a guide, who'll point out the plethora of trees and plants. Be sure to ask which ones are native to South Florida and which ones have been imported—Miami is a veritable breeding ground for exotics, from plants such as the yam vine to South American parrots.

Recently, the Safe Neighborhoods Parks Bonds has provided funds for reclamation and restoration of 8 acres of hardwood hammocks due to the over-abundance of the yam vine. When not controlled, this vine of African and Asian descent can deprive the light needed to encourage the growth of the tropical hardwood forest.

KEEP IN MIND
The park can be but a brief diversion. Fortunately, the Enchanted Forest with pony rides is adjacent. Otherwise, the area is rather commercial, with plenty of stores and restaurants. If it starts to rain, you can always escape to Loehmann's Plaza in Aventura, where a 24-screen multiplex theater and other activities provide indoor entertainment.

KID-FRIENDLY EATS Just a block or two away in the Arch Creek Plaza, **By Sarah's Café** (13200 Biscayne Blvd., tel. 305/893–0404) is a quaint, homey restaurant serving a mix of creative Italian, French, and American fare. Specialties such as duck salad, hot dogs, and grilled Reuben sandwiches are frequently on the lunch menu. Make sure you save room for dessert. The proprietors specialize in old-fashioned sweets, including pineapple upside-down cake.

BARNACLE STATE HISTORIC SITE

61

While this site may not interest kids under 4, older children will get an intriguing snapshot of what life was like here in the late 1800s and early 1900s. Ralph Middleton Munroe first came to Miami in 1877 for vacation, then settled here in 1882, shortly after his wife passed away. The Barnacle State Historic Site is the house he eventually built, and it is now considered the oldest home in Miami-Dade County in its original location.

Munroe originally built a boathouse on this 40-acre property so he could be near one of his beloved sailboats, the *Kingfish*. He lived in the boathouse until 1891, when the Barnacle was built. At the time it was a one-story structure built on wooden pilings, with an octagonal-shaped central room. Later, when he needed more room, the whole house was raised and a new story was inserted underneath, rather than on top of it.

The raising of the Barnacle began a new era in Munroe's life. He became well known for both the unusual shape of his home and for his yacht designs, and in 1887 he

KEEP IN MIND The Barnacle Site takes an hour or less to tour. Be sure to line up at the door of the Barnacle a few minutes before the tour times; once the tours start, no one will be allowed in. Afterward, stop by CocoWalk in nearby Coconut Grove for a bit of family shopping and people-watching fun.

HEY, KIDS! The "salvage business" used to be a polite phrase for causing boat wrecks and then profiting from them. Long ago, pirates in some areas used to lure boats intentionally onto dangerous reefs. Then, when the boats broke up, they'd wade into the surf and pick up the goods that floated in on the tide. Salvage can be a respectable business, though, if you're not personally responsible for the wreck, and even today companies who lose ships at sea contact salvage operators to raise their valuable cargo.

was elected Commodore of the Biscayne Bay Yachting Club, a position he would hold for 22 years. In 1894 he remarried and had two children, and in the years that followed made a fortune in the salvage business.

Many of his souvenirs are displayed at the house, including steam winches and pumps. His wealth allowed him to preserve the Barnacle's surrounding hammocks—tropical hardwood—which is one of the only surviving sites of the Miami Hammock. In addition to being a naturalist, Munroe was also a historian and photographer, and his efforts to preserve the *Era of the Bay* can be viewed throughout the site via sepia prints and antique furniture. All in all, this house is really a time capsule.

KID-FRIENDLY EATS Grab a quick plate of pasta next door at **Tuscany Trattoria** (3484 Main Hwy., tel. 305/445–0022), or some burritos and quesadillas at **Senor Frog's** (3480 Main Hwy., tel. 305/448–0999). If you continue walking for a block and make a left on Commodore Plaza, you'll find a pleasant outdoor café called **Greenstreet Café** (3110 Commodore Plaza, tel. 305/567–0662).

BASS MUSEUM OF ART

For kids interested in the arts, Miami has few better classical displays. This playful art deco–style museum contains possibly the most extensive collection of classical art in Miami, comprising historical and ecclesiastical paintings, sculptures, and textiles. Owing to the religious and adult nature of many of the 2,000 pieces, the collection will appeal most to children 14 and up, but younger ones will get a kick out of several of the museum's exhibits, especially the Egyptian mummy and its sarcophagus. The museum also routinely sponsors lectures, performances, and educational symposia.

The best way to see this museum is to request a guided tour. Volunteer docents happily interpret the hunts and celebrations of 15th-century Europe depicted in the wall-length textiles. They're also willing to expound on the history of the museum itself. The museum's permanent exhibit was gifted to the City of Miami Beach in 1963 by John and Johanna Bass. Born in Vienna, John was a successful businessman in New York, but he was also an accomplished musician, composer, painter, photographer, and inventor. His wife

KID-FRIENDLY EATS Only a block or so away, **Wolfie's** (2038 Collins Ave., tel. 305/538–6626) is a legendary deli that opened in 1947. Choices vary from matzoh ball soup to pancakes to corned beef sandwiches—in other words, something for everyone, unless you're a real stickler for dirt (the place isn't always the cleanest). If that's the case, head for nearby **Chow** (210 23rd St., tel. 305/604–1468), a beautifully designed pan-Asian place that's only open for dinner.

2121 Park Ave., South Beach

305/673-7530

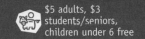 $5 adults, $3 students/seniors, children under 6 free

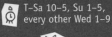 T–Sa 10–5, Su 1–5, every other Wed 1–9

 12 and up

Johanna was a poet and a pianist. They donated their collection on condition that the city would maintain it in perpetuity, provide for its exhibition, and keep it available to the public.

Much like the rest of South Beach's art deco gems, this building is listed on the National Registry. It has undergone recent renovations by Japanese architect Arata Isozaki, who has worked on projects for the Guggenheim Museum in New York and the Museum of Contemporary Art in Los Angeles. Apart from renovating the present 11,000 square ft, Isozaki has also added an additional 22,000 square ft to allow the museum to run a shop and café. And that's only Phase 1. Phase 2 plans will provide another 25,000 square ft for classrooms and an auditorium, in order to better serve the artistic-minded community. Grandiose is the South Beach way, and surely such an unusual collection deserves it.

KEEP IN MIND The plethora of nudes in both sculptures and oil paintings here may embarrass younger children, who might be better distracted in other parts of this cultural arts complex, such as the library or the new Miami City Ballet building.

HEY, KIDS! Just because you're good at one thing, doesn't mean you can't be good at another. Look at John Bass, the founder of this museum. He redefines the meaning of extracurricular activities. In fact, the only thing he didn't do, it seems, was hit a baseball out of the park. But he was probably willing to try.

BAYSIDE MARKETPLACE

Overlooking Biscayne Bay, this indoor-outdoor mall also doubles as an entertainment center. Although stores such as Disney and Warner Brothers and a plethora of souvenir kiosks will light up the eyes of all kids age 4 and up, the live music, ranging from Latin bands to groups of Caribbean drummers, is sure to enthrall kids and even inspire movement. Bayside, and the adjacent Bayfront Amphitheater, schedules musicians for almost every weekend of the year. Teens will no doubt enjoy the rock concerts and reggae festivals, featuring many marquee-quality performers such as Creed and Ziggy Marley.

Along with the musicians, street performers ranging from jugglers to magicians entertain kids of all ages. Some folks even walk around with their parrots and iguanas, then stop so kids can have their pictures snapped with them perched on their shoulders (for a small fee, of course). Babies might be a bit leery of reptiles and big, overly bright birds, but rest assured that these animals have sat on a lot of children's shoulders—they won't bite or peck unless your kid does it first.

KEEP IN MIND For sports-minded kids, a visit next door to the new American Airlines Arena, where the Miami Heat plays to sell-out crowds, should be a must-see. The Arena grounds are still in progress, but plans include outdoor recreational activities and playgrounds for children ages 2–5.

HEY, KIDS! The cruise ships look pretty big when they're docked, but wait until you spot 'em afloat: they look like entire cities on the move. All the big cruise lines dock here because Miami has a deep-water port, which is a port dug deep enough to accommodate large ships without grounding them. In addition to the cruise ships, lots of gigantic cargo ships unload their goods here. See if you can spot Dole swinging bananas ashore.

 401 N.E. Biscayne Blvd.,
Downtown Miami

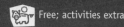 Free; activities extra

M–Th 10–10, F–Sa 10–11, Su 10–10

305/577–3344

 All ages

In addition to the eclectic sounds and people-watching, Bayside provides ample boating opportunities. You can take a trip on just about every kind of boat that docks here, from ferries to gondolas. A 10-year-old might prefer a ride on a speedboat, while a 5-year-old will find the slow, gentle motion of a small ferry fast enough.

Whatever their choice, they'll get a great close-up of the gigantic cruise ships that dock right across the bay, plus a look at several functioning drawbridges. The *Heritage of Miami II*, an 85-ft steel-topsail schooner, offers two-hour guided tours, which point out the houses of celebrities such as Gloria Estefan who live on the exclusive Star Island.

KID-FRIENDLY EATS

An elaborate food court on the second level sells everything from *churros* (a deep-fried pastry) to conch fritters. For a sit-down meal, the ever-popular **Los Ranchos** (401 N.E. Biscayne Blvd., tel. 305/376–0666) lavishes customers with terrific steaks, grilled South American–style and served with a virtual rainbow of sauces in lieu of ketchup.

BILL BAGGS CAPE FLORIDA STATE
RECREATION AREA

At this park, kids mix history with recreation. The 1.25-mi beach has, like its neighbor Crandon Park, some of the best beaches around for a variety of sand-and-surf fun. Even young anglers, casting a line off the seawall, will delight in some of the best shoreline saltwater fishing around. Snapper beware. Kids will enjoy the challenge of surf-fishing, where the pull and throb of the tide make for a very different experience than sinking a line in a calm, gentle lake.

Named after a newspaper editor who took a profound interest in restoring the natural resources of the region, this park is rich with history. Built in 1825 to guide ships over submerged reefs and sandbars, the Cape Florida Lighthouse stands at the southernmost tip of the park. In 1836, the structure was badly damaged by fire during the Second Seminole War, and remained out of service until 1842. The lighthouse was restored and relit in 1847, and its height was increased in 1855 from 65 to 95 ft. During the Civil War, its lights were smashed by Confederate soldiers; the lighthouse was later repaired and stayed in service

HEY, KIDS! You probably know all about mountain bikes and dirt bikes. Here in Miami, though, most of the kids grow up on water bikes. Some have motors—called Jet Skis—and some are like regular bicycles—called hydro-bikes—which are pedaled only in the water. Try out the last ones to see what it's like to ride in the ocean instead of on the ground.

until 1878. Finally, 100 years later, the U.S. Coast Guard restored the original lights to Cape Florida, and now the lighthouse is used as a navigational aid. Although a guided tour will explain its history, kids will get just as much of a thrill when going up the 118 steps to the top.

Aquatic recreation opportunities here are plenty. In addition to beach chairs and umbrellas, the concession stand rents ocean kayaks, Windsurfers, Jet Skis, and hydro-bikes, as well as sports equipment such as Rollerblades and bicycles. If your children would rather not risk the waves, which can be a trifle chilly in the winter months, take them for a ride along the Rickenbacker Causeway, a fixed bridge that spans the sparkling Atlantic Ocean from the mainland to the Keys. The stunning view from the highest point of the bridge will quiet even the chattiest kids, as they absorb the finest sights of nature.

KID-FRIENDLY EATS Eighteen covered pavilions provide shaded areas for picnicking. If you're picnic-basket-challenged, **The Lighthouse Café** (tel. 305/361-8487) in the park has plenty of tasty, child-enticing items for casual oceanfront munching. Just don't feed the pelicans; like sea gulls, they're pests who tend to overstay their welcome.

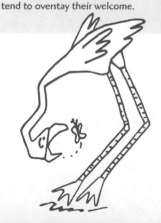

KEEP IN MIND If you're planning on saltwater fishing, you need to purchase a license for each member of the family who'll be casting a line. You can obtain licenses at any bait-and-tackle shop. Also, the Rickenbacker Causeway is a toll road, so be prepared to pay when you cross it on the way to the park.

BILL SADOWSKI PARK AND
NATURE CENTER

L ike many of Miami's parks, this one mostly caters to rough-and-tumble kids under the age of 5. If you start at the play area, toddlers can wear themselves out on the multitude of swings, slides, and monkey bars. Then you can lope the nature trails, which are fragrant with grasses and flowers, and wind up at the Interpretive Center. If ever a kid wanted to pet a turtle, this would be the place to do it, under the gentle guidance of the naturalists who work here. The center also keeps snakes, lizards, and other reptiles for viewing and occasional stroking.

By far the most popular activity is Star Viewing for Everyone. Astronomy was a passion for the park's namesake and this hammock boasts the darkest observing sky closest to Downtown Miami. Held every Saturday night throughout the year for free (8–10 PM, weather permitting), the Southern Cross Astronomical Society exercises a variety of large telescopes, allowing you to view all sorts constellations, planets, comets, and other

KEEP IN MIND The Southern Cross Astronomical Society sponsors free public telescope observations of the sun's surface from MetroZoo. Call 305/661–1375 for more information.

KID-FRIENDLY EATS Pack a late-night picnic for munching while you stargaze. If you're still hungry afterward, head out for burgers at **O'Casey's** (11415 S. Dixie Hwy., Pinecrest, tel. 305/256–2667), a roomy, modern Irish pub that pleases every age.

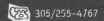
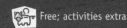

night-sky wonders. You can also bring your own telescopes and binoculars, in addition to blankets, lawn chairs, and bug repellent. Think of it as a natural fireworks show.

As pretty as the park is, the many programs make it more special. On the last Sunday of every month, the Earth Matters seminars show children different ways—such as recycling—to keep the Earth in top form and include hands-on projects. It's $4 per child, and those 8 and under must be accompanied by a parent. On every second Thursday, for $5 a person (ages 8 and up must be accompanied by a parent), children can learn about the nocturnal habits of local wildlife on a one-hour night walk along the nature trails. And for the little ones (ages 3–5), the park sponsors Mommy & Me and Daddy & Me classes in the nature center, so you can play with your children and learn about the environment simultaneously. Activities include games, crafts, walks, and stories.

HEY, KIDS! Sometimes you can see planets in the Miami skies without the aid of a telescope. How can you tell a planet from a star? It's easy. Planets tend to be bigger, brighter, and colored. For example, Mars glows red and Jupiter looks greenish. Occasionally, you can see a couple of planets in alignment, which means that they look like they're very close to each other.

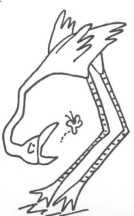

BILTMORE HOTEL

Hotels usually don't frighten children, but this one just might. Every week, the Miami Storytellers, a professional troupe, regales tales of the building's past by the fireside. Stories might include some real-life people who stayed at the Biltmore, including Ginger Rogers, Judy Garland, Bing Crosby, and gangster Al Capone, while others involve the injured soldiers who stayed at the Biltmore when it was a government-run hospital during World War II. Supposedly, the hotel is haunted by a few lost souls whose lives tragically ended here during the Great Depression. Nonetheless, tales are told in good fun and a complimentary glass of champagne is in it for the folks.

The building itself has quite a history, and kids will appreciate taking a tour of the gilded, marbled premises with hand-painted rafters. Coral Gables founder George E. Merrick designed the Biltmore in 1926 as a 26-story tower replica of the Giralda Tower in Seville, Spain. In its first heyday, during the Jazz Age of the 1920s, the hotel hosted aquatic events

HEY, KIDS! You're probably familiar with Tarzan, king of the jungle. But long before he was an animated movie star, Hollywood actors portrayed him. The most famous of these, Johnny Weismuller, was a swimming instructor at the Biltmore. He was also a swimming star who broke world records in the pool, all in preparation for setting a new one—the first Tarzan ever to swing from the trees.

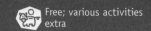

such as alligator wrestling and synchronized swimming, which were big Sunday-afternoon attractions.

After World War II, the Biltmore remained a VA hospital until 1968, when Coral Gables was granted ownership of the building. It stood vacant, however, until 1983, when a $55 million renovation was begun. Today, the Biltmore has the largest hotel pool in North America. Not only is it available for hotel guests, but local residents can take a dip when they buy a membership. You can even rent a poolside cabana for the day and relax in the lounge chairs shielded by bougainvilleas. The Biltmore is one of the premier resort hotels in the nation, as well as a structure on the National Register of Historic Places. Call ahead for reservations.

KID-FRIENDLY EATS The Biltmore has two restaurants on the premises: **La Palme D'Or** (tel. 305/445–1926) is a formal French eatery, but the **Courtyard Café** (tel. 305/445–1926) is more amenable to children and their likes and dislikes. On Sundays, take advantage of one of the premier brunch buffet spreads in the city.

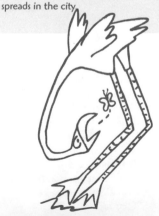

KEEP IN MIND Golf fans will want to try the hotel's 18-hole course—one of the best in South Florida. Book tee times well in advance. Since this course is extensive, young golfers can get fatigued playing 18 holes under the noonday sun. Plan to play only the first 9, or play twilight golf, which is not only less expensive but is accented by the gorgeous Florida sunset.

BISCAYNE NATIONAL PARK

T his 181,500-acre natural park is an expansive snapshot of the hidden world that covers more than 70% of the Earth's surface. In other words, we're talking about water—in this case the ocean. At first glance, it doesn't even look like a park. Yet most of this clear, shallow bay consists of submerged living coral reefs, which provide a home for an array of vibrantly colored aquatic life. The Miami area may be home to 14 artificial reef dive sites, but Biscayne National Park is one of the only all-natural sites.

This captivating ecosystem practically glows with color, half of which comes from the more than 200 tropical fish who feed on the reefs, including parrot fish, scorpion fish, angelfish, moray eels, and the enticingly named peppermint goby. Kids can view myriad underwater life either via a glass-bottomed boat tour or by guided snorkeling and diving. Aquatic photographers prefer this last option for better photo opportunities. You can also rent

KID-FRIENDLY EATS Homestead has plenty of eateries that cater to kids. Try the **White Lion Café & Antiques** (146 N.W. 7th St., tel. 305/248–1076), a rustic café with picnic tables on a porch and an interior dining room crammed with collectibles. Its homemade desserts are the most lovable sweets in Homestead.

KEEP IN MIND If you choose to dive or snorkel, remember that chillier air means even chillier water. You can rent wet suits and other diving/snorkeling equipment at the park or before you go. Snorkeling requires reservation times, as the park can get crowded. Also, be advised of wind and weather conditions before you leave Miami. If your tour is canceled because of bad weather, you can take advantage of downtown Homestead's antiques district, where you can browse for collectibles while the kids hold their ears at the nearby Motorsports Complex.

canoes, though it's harder to get a clear view of underwater life this way. Stop at the Convoy Visitor Center, at the entrance to the park, for more information.

If the kids are still craving for more, hike the short nature trail (about 30 minutes) on the mainland to learn more about the marine and bird life of the park. Kids will see the dense and impenetrable mangrove-dominated coastline, which not only protects the mainland during hurricanes but also provides young fish shelter from predators. Though these humped, misshapen trees appear as if they could star in their own Disney animated classic, the mangroves even help keep the waters of Biscayne Bay clean and free of muck by not permitting topsoil to wash past their roots into the water. Keep your eyes on the roots, and you'll see white ibis or snowy egret foraging for a light snack.

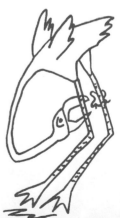

HEY, KIDS! Corals are not rocks but small animals related to jelly-fish. A coral reef is made up of thousands of the coral's external skeleton. Like humans, corals carefully choose where they build their reefs: water should be no more than 200 ft deep; a clean and well-lit area is required; and water temperature should be a perfect 68°F or above. And, of course, the right schools—of fish, that is—need to be close by. Only then will they consider a spot ideal for building.

BUTTERFLY WORLD

I t'd be accurate if you chanted "butterflies, butterflies everywhere" as you strolled through this exotic park. The fabulous winged creatures flit from flower to flower, filling the air with hues more varied than a rainbow. But then you'd neglect to mention the other wonderful aspects of this park, namely the busy hummingbirds and fat, satisfied fish.

Butterfly World, a collection of butterfly houses and aviaries in Tradewinds Park, is the largest butterfly house in the nation. Opened in 1988, it remains a favorite attraction throughout the region, appealing to all ages. Even finicky teens will appreciate the Tropical Rain Forest Aviary. Waterfalls mist the air in the 8,000-square-ft, screened-in rain forest, and kids can duck into shadowy caves.

Of course, the main attraction is the 5,000 butterflies. More than 80 species from South America and Asia flap their colorful wings here, including the owl and blue morpho butterflies. After viewing the exotics, check out the native butterflies that populate the expansive gardens. In the aromatic English Rose Garden and through clipped mazes and

HEY, KIDS! Butterflies and hummingbirds share a favorite food—the nectar they sip from flowers. Folks who want to plant butterfly gardens should grow not only pretty flowers but lots of green plants. Caterpillars, which eventually cocoon themselves and emerge later as butterflies, enjoy munching on leafy greens. So in order to ensure plenty of butterflies throughout the season, gardeners should allow caterpillars to build cocoons on the property near their food supply.

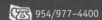 3600 W. Sample Rd., Coconut Creek

954/977–4400

 $10.95 adults,
$6 children 4–12

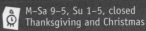 M–Sa 9–5, Su 1–5, closed
Thanksgiving and Christmas

 All ages

flowering passion vines of the Secret Garden, hundreds of indigenous species feed on the lavender nectar dripping from the Sky Vine. In the Jewels of the Sky Hummingbird Aviary, eight different species, the largest collection in the world, zip through the air alongside birds such as honeycreepers and brightly hued finches. Walk the suspension bridge, a less rickety copy of one found in Ecuador, to enter this particular aviary.

In 1998, Butterfly World opened its fifth aviary, the Lorikeet Encounter. Because lories and lorikeets tend to be personable and clownish parrots, they're great to introduce to kids under 4, who can feed them and pose with them for pictures. Since this is the final exhibit, it's an ideal way to end the tour when kids themselves get a little peckish.

KID-FRIENDLY EATS Because the attraction is inside the park, it's probably best to pack a picnic lunch and take advantage of the rest of the park's beauty after you exit Butterfly World. Otherwise, Sample Road provides plenty of fast-food options.

TRANSPORTATION Remember to look for Butterfly World inside Tradewinds Park, which is located 10 mi to the north of Fort Lauderdale. Take either the Florida Turnpike or Interstate I–95, exit at Sample Road, and head west. Enter the park on the south side of Sample Road, only a quarter of a mile west of the Florida Turnpike. The main butterfly house (the rain forest) is inside the park, straight ahead about a third of a mile.

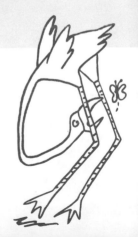

CHARLES DEERING ESTATE

This historic home will definitely impress kids, especially those studying American history. Charles Deering, brother of Vizcaya Museum builder James Deering, designed this main building of his Cutler Ridge compound—his winter home—in the Mediterranean Revival style, similar to the castles he owned in Spain. He called the 1922 building the Stone House, and used it to showcase his varied collection of woven tapestries, antique furnishings, rare books, and oil paintings of landscapes.

The 420-acre estate is more than just a novelty for vicariousness. The land itself is part of the Atlantic Coastal Ridge, a formation of 100,000-year-old oolitic limestone, which has yielded fossilized bones and teeth from mammoth, tapirs, jaguars, peccaries, sloths, and bison, among others. Archaeological human remains 10,000 years old have also been unearthed, which would place them at the time of the Paleo-Indians, some of the earliest indigenous peoples of North America. They were succeeded by the Tequesta Indians, who survived here until the late 18th century.

KEEP IN MIND For an additional fee, nature tours and half-day guided canoe tours are offered to the offshore island of Chicken Key, which is visible from the mainland. The lush beauty is definitely worth the trip.

HEY, KIDS! Richard Medlock, a local artist, carved a two-piece sculpture called "Wishing Stone" at the edge of the estate. One piece, called the "tidal stone," is in the shallow water right off the coast. During low tide only, you can view the carving on this stone as the remaining water trapped in it disappears through evaporation (which could take a couple of hours, depending on when you begin to observe the process). The result is magical enough to make you believe that if you make a wish while sitting on the adjacent second piece, called the "bench stone," it will indeed come true.

In 1838, the land was given to naturalist Dr. Henry Perrine and other well-known pioneers including Dr. William C. Cutler and Samuel H. Richmond. This first settlement of Miami gradually came to be called Cutler. Richmond grew locally famous for establishing the Richmond Cottage, a frame house that became the first hotel between Coconut Grove and Key West; the house remains a historic building on the site.

Now managed by Miami-Dade Park & Recreation Department, the Deering Estate offers, through hour-long guided tours, a multitude of opportunities to learn about the natural flora and fauna of Florida. Guides will help kids identify various rare plants including orchids, bromeliads, and ferns, and more than 40 species of trees, including huge live oaks, gumbo limbos, and pigeon plums. In addition, they'll help children spot a variety of wildlife such as gray foxes, spotted skunks, squirrels, bobcats, and birds that inhabit the area.

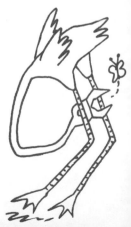

KID-FRIENDLY EATS The Deering Estate is about 40 minutes from downtown Miami. But if empty stomachs beckon on the way back to urban civilization, stop off at the **Old Cutler Inn** (78271 S.W. 168th St., Cutler Ridge, tel. 305/238–1514) for a bite of Southern home cooking. In Olde Cutler Town Center, a mini-mall, **Chopsticks House** (20553 Old Cutler Rd., Cutler Ridge, tel. 305/254–0080) satisfies hunger with its Chinese and Thai menus.

COCONUT GROVE FARMERS' MARKET

Don't you just love the activities that entertain as well as satisfy your taste buds? This popular Miami farmers' market attracts early risers, families, and curiosity-seekers to its wares on Saturday. Indeed, because the market starts so early in the morning, it's a great alternative to cartoons for the kids, and you can satisfy a thirst for fresh-squeezed juice at the same time. Plus, if you have a craving for Yukon gold potatoes or zebra-striped tomatoes, you've come to the right place. No, it's not a zoo, though the conglomeration of fruit-and-vegetable vendors can get busy enough to warrant the comparison.

Children of all ages love wandering through the many stalls, and not just because the exotic fruits and veggies are so colorful and unusual. Many of them, like key limes and mangos, come from the South Florida area; others, like akee fruit and dasheen, are imported from the Caribbean. In between the booths, vendors selling cinnamon rolls, fresh bread, or other baked goods often give out samples—at the very least, they perfume the

HEY, KIDS! You can tell when certain kinds of fruit are ripe by the way they feel. For example, peaches and pears get soft. Melons, like cantaloupes, should also feel a little soft, and the insides should sound loose and watery when you shake the fruit. Don't wait for apples to soften before you eat them, though—apples are one of the few fruits meant to be consumed when they're hard.

air with their delicious products. The cooked food that's available can range from Vietnamese spring rolls to French fries, and it's always possible to grab a thirst-quenching, freshly squeezed lemonade or a banana-strawberry smoothie.

While you shop for the week's groceries, potted plants, orchids, or fresh-cut flowers, wandering minstrel musicians strolling around the circumference of the market will entertain your children. Some clowns pull balloons into animal shapes, while others paint children's faces and arms with cool, colorful designs. This outdoor market, on a grassy knoll popular for year-round weekend festivals, is designed to keep the whole family occupied as well as rid itself of its products—and all before the sun gets too high in the sky and begins to wilt the lettuce.

KID-FRIENDLY EATS If the vendors selling sumptuous goodies don't fill up the tummies, walk up the street to perennial favorite **Johnny Rockets** (6769 Main St., tel. 305/827–0055) for milk shakes and burgers with everything on them.

KEEP IN MIND The produce here is vine ripened, which means that it's usually ready to eat immediately. That's the plus side. On the downside, ripe produce keeps ripening in the South Florida climate and tends to spoil quickly. You can slow rotting by putting ripe fruit in the refrigerator, with the exception of tomatoes, which will lose their flavor.

COCONUT GROVE PLAYHOUSE

One of the country's leading regional theaters, Coconut Playhouse presents superb modern theater and innovative interpretations of American family classics. Through enlightening and entertaining theater for both children and adults, the Playhouse is nationally recognized for its pursuit of artistic excellence.

The theater favors productions of Broadway revivals and musical revues, such as Andrew Lloyd Webber's "Song and Dance" and "Harry Chapin's America," which features the folk ballads of music legend Harry Chapin. The same high standards and originality apply equally to these productions as to its new works. Plays have featured such renowned celebrities as Kathleen Turner and Olympia Dukakis, and David Letterman hosted an on-the-road *Late Show* a couple of years ago. The theater hosts some matinees and, depending on the material, longer plays with intermissions.

Like many other of the country's playhouses, this one, built in 1926, began life as a movie theater and was transformed into a live theater in the mid-1950s. Two stages,

HEY, KIDS!

Pretend you're a theater critic. Take along a pad and pencil to the show. During the show or at intermissions, jot down what you like—or dislike—about the play and why. Don't forget the "why" part. That's what your opinion is based on.

KID-FRIENDLY EATS
A block or so away from the theater, **Mambo Café** (3105 Commodore Plaza, tel. 305/448–2768) dishes out some good, authentic Cuban cuisine at its sidewalk tables. Enjoy *vaca frita* (literally "fried cow") or shredded steak, while watching the crowd.

 3500 Main Hwy., Coconut Grove

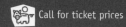 Call for ticket prices

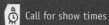 Call for show times

305/442–4000

 10 and up

the main one and the encore room, which is more like a lounge, will appeal to precocious children anxious to sample the adult world. The original Spanish rococo architecture has been preserved, and it resembles a tall frosted cake. The Playhouse is actually one of the few remaining historic sites in the Grove, and stands as tribute to the city's glamorous past.

Apart from a wide range of theater, the Playhouse also offers a variety of educational programs for all ages. Lizard Lessons, plays that explore practical life themes such as friendship and self-esteem, are performed for nearly 20,000 kindergarten through third-grade children each year. Other programs include A Summer Theater Camp for teens and Theater Stages, which explore playwriting, costumes, makeup, scenery, and other aspects of theater through ongoing classes.

KEEP IN MIND It's best to arrive a half hour prior to performances. For performance listings, see the *Miami Herald* weekend section. Be sure to exercise judgment when choosing a play to make sure it's age appropriate.

COCOWALK

Y ou'll have no problem occupying kids of all ages at this self-professed "heart and beat of the Grove." Nestled in the center of this formerly artistic, bohemian community, CocoWalk is a favorite hangout for local teens age 12 and up. In this three-story Spanish Mediterranean outdoor mall, kids like to drape themselves over the railings, watch the action below, and keep a lookout for like-minded friends. Fortunately, the mall is safe enough to leave your kids by themselves for a limited time, since the area also teems with adults and security personnel.

If you can restrict your kids to just looking, wandering around in the variety of popular shops (Gap, Banana Republic, etc.) will surely pique their interest. In the courtyards, kiosks display everything from T-shirts to hair clips. Other stands sell gourmet coffee and ice cream. Set your kids up with a sundae, take a seat on the stone steps, and listen to the live bands that frequently play here. Recent musicians have included Spanish guitar virtuoso Arturo Fuerte and dancer Erika Denz, who demonstrates the intricacies of the samba and other Brazilian dances.

KID-FRIENDLY EATS
The ever-popular **Cheesecake Factory** (3015 Grand Ave., tel. 305/447–9898) delights children of all ages with huge slices of more than 20 different kinds of its namesake sweets, not to mention salads, sandwiches, and pastas. For a real Miami experience, get in line for **Café Tu Tu Tango** (2977 McFarlane Rd., tel. 305/529–2222), a Miami-based minichain where all portions are appetizer size and live artists paint their original artwork while you eat.

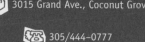 3015 Grand Ave., Coconut Grove

 Free

 Daily 10–10

305/444–0777

 All ages

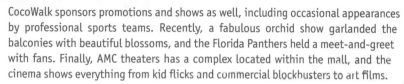

CocoWalk sponsors promotions and shows as well, including occasional appearances by professional sports teams. Recently, a fabulous orchid show garlanded the balconies with beautiful blossoms, and the Florida Panthers held a meet-and-greet with fans. Finally, AMC theaters has a complex located within the mall, and the cinema shows everything from kid flicks and commercial blockbusters to art films.

Coconut Grove is not only home to outdoor malls but to outdoor festivals. Some of the biggest include Taste of the Grove, when area restaurants set up kiosks and live bands play, and the Coconut Grove Arts Festival, a juried show that attracts artists and connoisseurs from all over the world. For event listing, check the *Miami Herald* weekend section.

HEY, KIDS! Coconut Grove was originally home to a group of Bahamians. The Bahamas, along with Cuba, are actually the closest Caribbean islands to the United States. Today, the Bahamians and the Cubans are two of the largest ethnic groups in Miami.

KEEP IN MIND Although CocoWalk and Coconut Grove proper are safe to walk around, other nearby neighborhoods can be a little dangerous for people of all ages. Remind kids to stick to well-lighted areas and crowded places for safety reasons, avoid walking down shadowed streets or away from the open businesses, avoid prolonged conversations with strangers, and never go anywhere by themselves.

CORAL CASTLE OF FLORIDA

This unusual castle will no doubt interest kids, especially those under 10. For two decades in the early 20th century, an immigrant from Latvia named Edwarde Leedskalnin carved this castle from coral rock using old-fashioned hand tools such as chisels. He did it to impress his 16-year-old fiancée, who left him the night before their wedding.

It didn't work. The fiancée didn't return to marry Leedskalnin. But in the end, it didn't seem to matter, for he had this new obsession to keep him happy—once the castle itself was built, he went on to furnish it. Today, in the courtyard, you can see his remarkable coral chairs. He also decorated the place with working fountains, birdbaths, and sundials, not to mention a telescope that's aimed at the North Star.

To some, coral rock sounds like an oxymoron—two completely different things. After all, coral is what reefs are made of. In places like Miami, however, where the earth and the

HEY, KIDS!

Coral rock is now considered an illegal building material. It can't be mined or taken from the sea. So the only way you can have a house built of coral is to buy one that already exists. But most people who live in them don't want to give them up because they are so rare.

KEEP IN MIND Depending on whom you ask, you'll get opinions on this attraction ranging from pretty interesting to pointless. The good news is, once you're down in Homestead, you can always take off for the high-decibel Miami-Dade Homestead Motorsports Complex, go antiquing on Krome Avenue, or hit the U-pick farms for a little fresh produce and a lot of fresh dirt.

ocean are at the same level, the coral from the sea was embedded into the land. The only way to get it out was to dig for it, as you would with coal or diamonds. And like coal or diamonds, coral rock has always been considered a very valuable material.

Still, the mystery here has nothing to do with either geography or the builder's professed love. It's more along the lines of the Egyptian pyramids: no one knows quite how one man single-handedly and with no modern machines moved 1,000 tons of coral— the amount required by the castle and its furnishings. Engineers assume that he used a rope-and-pulley system, but even they're still boggled by how he managed to hang a 9-ton coral gate that you can push open with your little toe.

KID-FRIENDLY EATS Homestead is known for its authentic Mexican cuisine, which you can sample at **El Toro Taco** (1 S. Krome Ave., tel. 305/245–8182) or at **Casita Tejas** (27 N. Krome Ave., tel. 305/248–8224); both restaurants win raves from local residents.

CRANDON PARK BEACH & FAMILY
AMUSEMENT CENTER

Miami prides itself on fine beaches, and Crandon Park is one of the 10 best beaches in the United States. This 2-mi stretch of white sand is protected by an offshore sandbar, which reduces surf and provides pleasantly calm waters, perfect for babies or toddlers who like to splash in the shallows. Older kids can swim out to the sandbar, in plain view of the 13 lifeguard towers, for a little privacy from the folks. A promenade winds up and down the beach, which makes for a great stroll.

For an energetic respite from the beach, check out the colorful carousel at the Family Amusement Center. Built in 1949, this recently restored, hand-painted treasure is the center's focal point. Prop a youngster on *Pretty Phoebe*, painted with dolphins and butterflies, for a quick whirl. Or saddle a young 'un up on *Danny Boy*, whose decor includes pirates. Then set them free to whirl in the moist sunshine to old-fashioned organ music.

For the older kids, the outdoor roller rink, commanded mostly by hockey-style Rollerbladers, is a great outlet for energy. A splash fountain in the shape of a dolphin and several hands-

KEEP IN MIND The parking lot has enough space for 3,000 vehicles, so don't get discouraged if it looks crowded. This beach and park is one of the most visitor-friendly in the area. Remember to bring plenty of sunscreen. The summer sun is brutal and the winter sun can still pack a wallop. The burn potential starts to increase in March, when the angle of the sun is similar to that of the late summer.

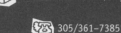

on marine animal sculptures amuse the little ones while the older kids whiz around the rink.

Nature-minded kids shouldn't miss the opportunity to tour the Crandon Park Gardens, founded on the site of the old zoo. The 200-plus-acre gardens contain a variety of botanical treats, including a lush, overgrown rain forest with winding pathways and dripping foliage. Other trails lead through tropical hardwood areas, where wildlife is easily observed. Conclude a hike with a canoe trip across one of the lakes in the formal part of the gardens called Central Garden.

Lastly, rest your muscles and let the tour guides do the work on the Tropical Jungle Hayride. The half-hour trip takes place only on Saturday from 10 to 1, and is a grand opportunity to hear about Key Biscayne's exciting past of pirates and coconut plantations.

HEY, KIDS! Stay clear of the man-of-wars, which look like blue balloons, lying on the beach. Although they look fascinating, these creatures occasionally wash up on shore and will sting you if you touch them. If you see one floating in the water, just swim away from it, head back to shore, and tell the lifeguard.

KID-FRIENDLY EATS The park provides plenty of picnic areas with grills. Alternatively, the concession stands dotting the beach provide burgers and hot dogs—plus ice cream, of course. If you're willing to sacrifice your parking spot, head to **La Carreta** (12 Crandon Blvd., tel. 305/365–1177) for Miami's edible identity: Cuban black beans and rice, plus a host of other specialties such as shredded steak or chicken with yellow rice.

CRANDON PARK TENNIS CENTER

Interested tennis fans and budding tennis pros alike will thoroughly enjoy this outing. Apart from taking in the pristine surroundings, families can play where the pros play. Such supercelebs as Venus Williams, Pete Sampras, and Andre Agassi have all played hot matches on these courts. And for youngsters wanting to learn, a better place to teach tennis is hard to find.

The stadium easily impresses with numbers: 7,500 permanent seats, an additional 6,500 temporary seats for tournaments, 16 stadium entrances (and 16 matching rest rooms), and 32 televisions in the inner and outer concourse all demand attention. But the real stars here are the courts—17 Laykold cushioned hard courts, 6 lighted for evening play; 8 state-of-the-art clay courts, 4 with red European clay and 4 with green American clay;

KID-FRIENDLY EATS
Open every day, **Sundays on the Bay** (5420 Crandon Blvd., tel. 305/361–6777) combines an ocean view with appetizing fare. Though there's no kids' menu, the appetizers serve nicely as a meal for any child who loves fried food.

HEY, KIDS! Tennis players speak their own language. For example, "let" means a ball hit the net during a serve. If you score an "ace," that means your opponent couldn't return your serve, and you win the point. And "love" means a score of zero unless, of course, the person you're playing is your mom or dad. Then love takes on a new double meaning.

7300 Crandon Blvd.,
Key Biscayne

305/365–2302

Hard courts: $3 adults per hr daily, $5 per hr nightly; children $2 per hr daily, $3 per hr nightly. Clay courts: $6 adults per hr, $3 children per hr

Daily 8–10, no evening play on clay courts

8 and up

and 2 grass courts—all open to the public. You can bet kids will thrill to the idea of playing where the top power hitters of the day have played.

Fortunately, your children don't have to be world-class players to spend time on these courts. Individual private or semiprivate lessons are available daily, from one of six USPTA- or USPTR-certified staff instructors. Tennis and fitness classes run on Tuesday and Thursday, 9:30–11:30. If you're visiting during May, the Florida Tennis Association Young Guns Jr. Tennis Classic holds its annual tournament and always provides exciting matches. Top players, ages 12–14, from around the state compete, and it's a great opportunity for kids to see where and how the medal winners begin. Who knows, your kids may see tomorrow's tennis superstar.

KEEP IN MIND The center is adjacent to the Crandon Park Beach and Family Amusement Center, so an hour of play here can be a brief side trip. It's also right next door to the Crandon Park Golf Course, one of the top 75 municipal golf courses in the country. Follow up tennis play with a little tee off, and you'll have some pleasantly exhausted kids on hand.

DAVE & BUSTER'S

Not many kids, or adults, can resist Dave & Buster's. The 58,000-square-ft place is dedicated solely to entertaining, and contains a zillion games ranging from arcade and virtual reality to billiards.

Start your gaming at the front desk, where you can sign up for pocket billiards tournaments and shuffleboard tables. At the 19th Hole, you can practice your golf swing or teach your child the right way to hold a club. This golf simulator allows you to tee off and putt on virtual reality greens. In the rear of the facility, batting cages prepare your kids for Little League. Next, you can sharpen your shot at the Chicago Shootout, which was designed after a 1920's speakeasy, or improve your laser-beam aim as you engage in a futuristic fight for your rights in the Ground Zero room.

The Million Dollar Midway is perhaps the most extensive attraction, with a plethora of video and arcade games. The Midway boasts the latest in simulator technology, which may be too advanced for children under 8. Kids can win tickets when they play arcade

HEY, KIDS! Billiards, or pool, is as much about math as it is about shooting balls into pockets. In fact, the best billiards players have a keen understanding of geometry, a type of mathematics that teaches about angles. To shoot a ball into a hole, you need to know what the angle is and where to hit the ball to make it do what you want.

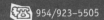

games and you can redeem them for prizes at the Winner's Circle (stuffed animals always rank among the favorites). Nostalgic parents will also appreciate the opportunity to play dinosaur video games such as Galaga and Pac-Man, not to mention a whole line of pinball machines.

Though toddlers are obviously too young to take advantage of interactive gaming technology, even 1- and 2-year-olds love the D&B Speedway. Formula 1 race cars, stock cars, and motocross bikes are intended for simulated racing, but the little ones adore sitting in the cars and on the motorcycles, pushing buttons and watching the screens flash. Parental supervision is necessary, of course, to make sure the youngsters don't fall off. In addition, the best time to allow young children to clamber on and off the machines is during the daytime hours, when competition for the simulators is at a minimum, and there's plenty of racing—virtual or just plain pretend—to go around.

KEEP IN MIND

Some of the video, arcade, and virtual reality games here can be violent, noisy, or inappropriate for certain ages. Parental guidance is a good idea. You especially might want to steer your kids clear of the Electric Chair simulator, a graphic display that some find amusing and others find horrifying.

KID-FRIENDLY EATS The restaurant at Dave & Buster's is not only full service, but it's worth the trip to the complex just to munch on battered chicken fingers, tangy Buffalo wings, gourmet pizzas, and baby-back ribs. If you're interested in breakfast, stop at the neighboring **Starlite Diner** (3500 Oakwood Blvd., tel. 954/924–2012), a stainless-steel contraption that can look almost otherworldly at night, when it glows like the moon.

ENCHANTED FOREST ELAINE
GORDON PARK

Although this nature preserve attracts fitness-inspired locals to its jogging/biking trail, which borders hardwood hammocks, bisects seasonal wetlands, and rims the Arch Creek Canal, kids of all ages undoubtedly come here for the pony rides.

On busy days and weekends, the staff keeps about a half dozen ponies saddled and in the ring, ready to be led on as many laps as the parent wants to pay for (about $1 per lap, with bargains like eight laps for $5). Other ponies rest in a neighboring corral, occasionally coming up to the fences for a stroke or pat on the nose. Others may just prefer to feed in the stalls or get groomed in the stables. Kids will get a good sense of the care that's involved in keeping—not just riding—a pony.

For a little respite from the sun, duck into the forest. Although the bike path is unpaved, the nature trail is a wide expanse of asphalt—perfect for strollers and wheelchairs. You

HEY, KIDS!
The nature preserve contains some poisonous plants. Do not under any circumstances eat berries or fruit off bushes or trees, no matter how enticing they may look—they could make you very ill.

KEEP IN MIND As in all parks and preserves, no alcoholic beverages are allowed, and fires may only be built in barbecue pits only. In addition, no plants or animals may be collected in the park or removed from the park, and if you want to bring the family dog to play Frisbee, call first—most don't allow pets (but some beaches do at certain times).

can wander through pine ridges and mangrove hammocks, identify saw palmettos, fig groves, and wild coffee plants, and basically bask in the pine-scented shade.

The nature trail leads to two playgrounds in the southwest corner of the park. The first is challenging for kids 6 and up, with monkey bars and a climbing apparatus, not to mention long slides. The second, designed for youngsters under 6, contains toddler-size climbing toys, slides, benches, and corrals for playing "horsie." A colorful spinning globe stands in the middle of this playground; see if your kids can find Florida.

Plenty of rest rooms and picnic shelters are scattered through the preserve, the latter being especially handy during unexpected summer rains. Information boards throughout the park identify plants and wildlife to view, so remind kids to keep a watchful eye open.

KID-FRIENDLY EATS The Enchanted Forest is an ideal picnic spot, but it's also just off Biscayne Boulevard (next to Arch Creek Park), which offers plenty of lunching and dining opportunities. Take stock at **Boston Market** (12500 Biscayne Blvd., tel. 305/892–8867) for chicken and corn bread, or take it with you to the park.

EQUESTRIAN CENTER
AT TROPICAL PARK

Its enthusiasm for horses notwithstanding, this park provides plenty of fun-filled activities that will amuse and excite both children and parents alike. The Equestrian Center celebrates the equine, and those who have an affinity for the equine, by presenting more than 30 horse competitions during a single season. Owners display prize-winning breeds, such as Arabians and hunter/jumpers, and fiercely compete for blue ribbons and show trophies, reminding spectators that horse-showing is serious business.

Formerly a racetrack, the center has two sand show rings, one for competition and the other for warm-ups and cool-downs. In the latter, children will get a close-up of the horses in a more relaxed atmosphere; the former show ring is highly charged with energy and makes for more exciting viewing. From there, kids can examine the two grass courses and gawk at the two-story judging booths. Call ahead for show times. The center also sponsors rodeos, which tend to draw large crowds. Fortunately, portable bleachers add about 9,000

HEY, KIDS! Not only do local police ride horses, they also ride bikes. On the beach, they sometimes drive sand buggies; if you pay close attention, you might even see a few Rollerblading in full uniform. A couple of years ago, the police force on Miami Beach was required to take lessons in order to keep up with the bad guys, many on Rollerblades themselves.

7900 S.W. 40th St., West Miami-Dade

 305/554-7334

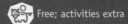 Free; activities extra

 Daily 7–10

 All ages

seats to the permanent 1,000. Children can also view the stables, where the mounted police units of Miami-Dade keep their partners.

Apart from the horses, this extensive park is filled with other amenities, including tennis, racquetball, basketball courts, and playing fields for soccer and baseball. Family activities range from sailing to paddleboating on the largest of the four lakes. Fishing is also permitted in the lake on the park's north side, which is kept stocked with largemouth bass, bluegill, and catfish. In fact, the Urban Fishing Program, designed to give children a chance to learn about the joys of fishing, was begun in this park in 1990. And finally, little ones will adore the two elaborate play centers. Horse fans or not, the park is a tropical paradise just waiting for visitors to take advantage.

KEEP IN MIND
Each year the Equestrian Center is closed from November to mid-January to make way for "Santa's Enchanted Forest," a Christmas-theme park with trees entwined with thousands of tiny lights, numerous rides, and multitudes of arcade games. It's also one of the largest temporary shows in the nation.

KID-FRIENDLY EATS The strip malls across the street provide plenty of fast food. For something more delectable, **Tropical Chinese Restaurant** (7991 S.W. 40th St., tel. 305/262-1552), a world-class Hong Kong–style eatery, serves tasty dumplings and noodle dishes. On Saturday and Sunday, an extensive dim sum meal—which is a lot of little appetizers—is rolled around on carts. Kids will get a kick out of picking out what they want without having to move.

EVERGLADES ALLIGATOR FARM

Alligators and crocodiles of all sizes teem in the ponds and pens at this not-so-ordinary farm, on the edge of Everglades National Park. But there's more here than just 'gators. John Hudson initially started the alligator farm as an airboat ride attraction in 1982, and it's still one of the farm's major enticements to experience the unspoiled Everglades.

43

The narrated airboat tours last about 30 minutes, and will thrill kids over the age of 4. The tour guides give you life jackets and cotton for your ears—airboats are quite loud—and steer you into the canals where your children will see myriad wildlife in their natural habitat. Watch for large waterbirds such as herons and osprey, plus turtles, water snakes, tarpon and bass, and even alligators. The alligators like to float quietly near the surface, camouflaged by the vegetation, and wait for prey. Remember to keep your hands in the boat.

HEY, KIDS!

Did you know alligators can grow about 3 ft a year? That means a 1-year- old baby alligator is about the same size as a 3-year-old child. An easy way to tell a baby alligator from an adult alligator is by its stripes. All alligators are born with stripes, which disappear over time, and aren't considered fully grown until they lose them.

KEEP IN MIND In addition to alligators and crocodiles, the Everglades is host to 50 other species of reptiles. Twenty-seven kinds of snakes, 16 species of turtles, and 15 different amphibians lurk about, the most common sightings being the Florida water snake, the striped mud turtle, and the Florida cricket frog. Be aware, though, that the canals and Everglades contain some poisonous species, such as the Florida cottonmouth and dusky pigmy rattlesnake. Make sure children keep their hands to themselves.

40351 S.W. 192 Ave., Homestead

 $12.50 adults,
$6 children 4–12

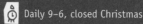 Daily 9–6, closed Christmas

 All ages

305/247–2628

Back at the farm, peruse the crocodile pond for the North American crocodile (like the one in Peter Pan) and the South American caiman (a smaller but no less fierce variety), or check out the spine-tingling snake shows. But the biggest attraction, of course, is the alligators. The breeding ponds contain the biggest specimens, which can grow as long as 14 ft. The hatcheries keep the eggs in temperature-controlled incubators and, depending on your luck, you may witness a birth, which is similar to a chicken pecking its way out of an egg. In the grow-out pens, alligators range from a few months to 4 years. Visit the breeding ponds, hatcheries, and grow-out pens, in that order.

The breeding projects were begun in 1985 in order to replenish the American alligator, which at the time was nearly extinct. Today, however, over 1.5 million alligators exist in the wild—and the not-so-wild—and have been removed from the endangered list. Indeed, during mating season, many South Florida residents find lovelorn alligators in their backyards in search of mates.

KID-FRIENDLY EATS Hot dogs and ice cream are available at the snack bar, as well as "gator nuggets," which are fried pieces of alligator tail. For something more substantial, try **The Pit Bar-B-Q** (16400 S.W. Tamiami Trail, Miami, tel. 305/226–2272), a self-serve barbecue joint, for smoky blackwood-oak-barbecued pork and beef ribs—a hands-on treat for kids dying to touch something that doesn't bite back.

EVERGLADES CITY TO TEN THOUSAND ISLANDS

Looking for a day trip of wildlife viewing, airboat rides, and boat tours? This aquatic outpost, just 83 mi from Miami, provides families with an activity-filled day away from the hustle and bustle of the city. Your first stop, however, should be at the Gulf Coast Visitor Center (Rte. 29, tel. 941/695–3311) to collect information about the types and rates of various excursions.

A 19th-century community, Everglades City is the only entrance to the watery depths of the Everglades National Park and Ten Thousand Islands, a group of tiny islands and their estuaries. If your children are passive participants, book passage on the Everglades National Park Boat Tours (tel. 800/445–7724). A narrated 1½-hour trip with a naturalist takes you through the Ten Thousand Islands, with plenty of chances to glimpse—or outright stare—at teeming wildlife in its natural habitat.

HEY, KIDS! It's easy to paddle a canoe when you hold the paddle the right way. After pulling it through the water, bring the paddle up and turn it sideways so that the blade is flat. This is called feathering, which helps prevent the wind from slowing you down by putting resistance on the paddle as you bring it forward. Then, when you reach the front of your swing, dip it again into the water with the blade perpendicular to the boat and pull. You'll be amazed how swiftly your canoe will move through the water.

 3 mi south of U.S. 41 (Tamiami Trail) on CR 29, north side of Chokoloskee Bay,

 n/a

 Free; activities extra

 n/a

 All ages

For a more exhilarating sweep inside and outside the Everglades, try an airboat or a swamp buggy ride. Wooten's Everglades Adventures (tel. 941/695–2781) offers a variety of excursions, and Jungle Erv's Airboat World (tel. 941/695–2805) gives group and private airboat tours and offers jungle tours on much quieter pontoon boats.

For adventure-seeking kids 10 and older, journey to the islands by canoe. The trip from the north shore of Chokoloskee Bay can be hard work, but the payoff is worth it. The Ten Thousand Islands form myriad passes and miniature bays, with islands for overnight camping. Keep in mind, though, that the islands open up to the Gulf of Mexico. The wisest choice, even for experienced paddlers, is to hire a guide or join a tour of the area via North American Canoe Tours (tel. 941/695–4666), who guide from November to April.

KID-FRIENDLY EATS The **Rod and Gun Club** (200 Riverside Dr., Everglades City, tel. 941/695–2101) serves up plenty of fresh seafood amid dark wood walls adorned with hunting and fishing trophies. Or stop in at **Susie's Station** (103 S.W. Copeland Ave., Everglades City, tel. 941/695–2002), which displays antique cars and also sells local seafood and homemade key lime pie.

KEEP IN MIND If you're planning a day trip to the 'glades, stock a travel bag with necessities: bottled water, snacks, binoculars, sunscreen, insect repellent, hats, and long-sleeve shirts. Whatever excursion you choose, be sure you check the weather forecast before you set out. Though the skies may be postcard perfect in Miami, the Everglades could be suffering storms. If you're planning to camp, you'll need a permit, which the Gulf Coast Visitor Center provides at no charge.

FAIRCHILD TROPICAL GARDENS

41

The largest botanical garden in the United States, this 83-acre park is devoted to plants from tropical regions around the globe. A bouquet of colors and aromas unfolds from the more than 5,000 plants maintained here. Plenty of palms and exotic trees dot the landscape, and 11 ponds and lakes provide fodder for waterbirds ranging from great blue herons to ducks.

Tram rides are the best way to experience the gardens, with narrated tours that last about 40 minutes. Children age 4 and under, who might not be interested in the narrative, will be soothed by the motion of the electric tram. Older kids, especially those ages 8–12, will learn the history of the tropical gardens and its variety of plant life. Once back at base, you can take a guided walking tour or roam around the paved path on your own. All plants are labeled, and visitors are welcome to touch, smell, and even talk to the trees and flowers—as long as they don't pick them.

KID-FRIENDLY EATS Although you can't bring a picnic into the gardens, **Matheson Hammock Park** is right next door and you can enjoy a packed lunch there. Otherwise, head into nearby Coral Gables for macaroni-and-cheese or stupendous meat loaf at the **Gables Diner** (2320 Galiano St., tel. 305/567–0330).

HEY, KIDS! Though you may be tempted to run and play on the grassy fields and splash around in the lakes, this is one place where you have to follow the rules. You can explore, just be careful of where you step—you wouldn't want to crush a rare or endangered plant. While you're at the gardens, try winding your tongue around the Latin names of the plants. Most adults won't even know how to pronounce them.

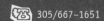 10901 Old Cutler Rd., Miami

305/667-1651

$8 per person,
children under 13 free

Daily 9:30–4:30, closed Christmas

All ages

A sunken garden near the entrance will fascinate toddlers who like hidden places, though they may need a little assistance clambering around here. For budding young scientists, a collection of the world's smallest tropical plants actually require magnifying glasses to see them (inquire at the gift shop for glasses). But be sure to hold the plants at an angle that doesn't catch the light, so you don't accidentally burn them up!

Kids who like vibrant colors should especially note the orchids, the brilliantly hued flowers that seemingly live on air, hence their designation as "air plants," which are plants that grow on other plants rather than in the ground. They'll appreciate the abundant bougainvillea, which have as many blooms as a Pokémon collector has cards. The gardens also displays rare plants when they come into season. An actual rain forest takes advantage of the native humidity, which means you don't have to travel to South America to experience the jungle.

KEEP IN MIND Like many South Florida attractions, the botanical gardens are almost completely outdoors. If rain is threatening or it's unusually hot, save the tour for another day. Although countless trees provide abundant shade, summertime strolling can lead to heat fatigue and whiny kids. The most ideal time to visit the gardens is in the winter (November–April), when the skies are clear and the flowers are in bloom.

FLAMINGO PARK AND TENNIS CENTER

4O

It's time to pack a picnic basket, and enjoy an activity-filled day in the warm South Florida sun! The only full-service park in South Beach, Flamingo has a something-for-everyone feel. For young children, a large playground contains swings, slides, and bright plastic jungle gyms. The park is also a pleasure patch for the resident pooches, and since plenty of kids birthday parties take place here, you might even spot the occasional pony making the rounds.

After your kids have cuddled with enough dogs, check out the basketball and racquetball courts and soccer fields for a pick-up game. If nothing's available, head over to the tennis center. Flamingo grooms about 16 clay courts and two hard courts for competitive play. Kids can also sign up for group or individual lessons here, while parents play at the next court. Parent-child matches are also frequent scenes here. On the northwest side of the park, a baseball field is often the site for local league games. A tennis stadium hosts

TRANSPORTATION Since it's so hard to find a parking space on South Beach, don't risk losing yours. Consider renting bicycles from the concessions on Ocean Drive and coasting the eight or so blocks down to the park for some well-earned rest and relaxation.

Michigan Ave. and 14th St.,
South Beach

305/673-7765

Free

Daily 8-sunset

All ages

junior tournaments on the other side, and a soccer field, surrounded by a track, helps Miami's male and female semipro teams finesse their game.

Unless you're actively playing a sport, a trip to this park won't take more than an hour. Plan on going to the beach or using the park as a break between exploring the art deco strip of Ocean Drive or strolling the walking mall on Lincoln Road.

South Beach also has two other parks. Lummus Park borders the beach and is primarily used for a beachside soccer game or a concert. South Pointe Park, a waterside wedge of land overlooking Government Cut, is great for viewing the cruise ships slide into the Atlantic Ocean from the port, but can be overcrowded. Of the three, Flamingo is both the cleanest and the safest for kids.

KEEP IN MIND
Don't plan on visiting the park at night, unless you're signed up for a tennis court. The place changes character after dark, and while not exactly dangerous, it's best avoided.

KID-FRIENDLY EATS Most kids like hot dogs, but don't know much about knockwurst, which are really only bigger hot dogs. Educate them at **Dab Haus** (852 Alton Rd., tel. 305/534-9557), a German restaurant that is a favorite among the locals.

GOLD COAST RAILROAD MUSEUM

orget all you know about replica train sets and head to this museum, one of the oldest in Miami, for the real thing. Displayed on a half mile track, these life-size historic railroad cars put miniatures to shame. Young railroad buffs will delight in the authentically restored engines, Pullmans (sleeping cars), and dining cars that have been kept here since 1957. And yes, all the cars are in working condition. The price of admission includes a ride on the Edwin Link Children's Railroad, a real thrill for children under 5.

For kids 5 and up, who may be into collecting model trains, the 1948 *Silver Crescent* dome car is of special interest. The round-ended car was one of seven attached to the rear of the *California Zephyr*, a train considered the most modern at the time. It even had central air-conditioning. As you tour the *Silver Crescent*'s porter stations, private cabins, and lounges, you'll hear the "Zephyrette" hostess make announcements about points of interest and dining times. Songs and commercials of the era—'50s and '60s—also play over the sound system.

HEY, KIDS!

Miami has several working railroad tracks, so you may actually see some live trains in action. Of course, it's not always fun to get caught at a light by a cargo train, which can be very, very long. To entertain yourself, see if you can count the cars as they lumber past.

KEEP IN MIND

Touring takes 45 minutes or so. The museum is a frequent destination for school field trips, so call ahead to make sure it is open to the public. The trains make for a good side trip, but the car trip down to southwest Miami-Dade can be a little long if this is a destination unto itself. You may want to include a visit to the adjacent MetroZoo.

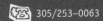 12450 S.W. 152 St., Miami

305/253-0063

 $5 adults, $3 children under 12

M-F 11–3, Sa–Su 11–4

All ages

Even kids who have little interest in trains will find it hard not to be impressed by the *Ferdinand Magellan*. This is the only Pullman car specifically constructed for U.S. president Franklin Delano Roosevelt in the 1930s. Other presidents who have ridden in it include George Bush, Dwight Eisenhower, Ronald Reagan, and Harry S Truman.

In 1992, the *Ferdinand Magellan* was damaged by Hurricane Andrew, but has since been completely restored by a team of experts from the Smithsonian Institute. Other cars and train sheds are still under construction. Soon, like the *Ferdinand Magellan*, all the cars on site will be shining examples of National Historic Landmarks, as well as an indication of how luxuriously our presidents are treated.

KID-FRIENDLY EATS The nearby MetroZoo has plenty of fast-food-style stands and restaurants; otherwise, road trips may be in order. You can sample some fun, wacky diner fare at **K.C. Cagney & Co.** (11230 S.W. 137th Ave., Kendall, tel. 305/386–1555) or order cheeseburgers by the ounce at **Cheeburger Cheeburger** (11531 S.W. 88th St., Kendall, tel. 305/596–1211). And don't skimp on the onions rings and milk shakes.

GREYNOLDS PARK

B ecause Oleta River State Recreation Area is close by, this park and nature preserve sometimes goes unnoticed, which is a shame, since 160 acres of its lushly landscaped hills, a former stomping ground for the Tequesta Indians, are ideal for children of all ages. Indeed, the hardwood hammocks and pine flatwoods form quite the oasis from busy city life, which lies just outside the entrance.

Picnic areas are close to playgrounds, so parents can set up their foodstuffs while the little ones play on the jungle gyms. Those a bit older will want to take off promptly for the hilltop castle or stone fort, which dates from the 1930s. The path leading up to it is rocky and can be tricky, so parents might want to accompany the kids to this mini Camelot. Just don't leave your food unattended—raccoons, squirrels, and birds just might help themselves.

The park is well known for its bird rookery (a breeding place), which at one time housed about 3,000 wading birds. Though some critics say the rookery has been depleted by

HEY, KIDS! Look around near the water, and no doubt you'll spot some big, black birds perched on tree limbs. They'll appear frozen in position, with their wings outstretched. No, they're not about to pounce on something. These birds, called anhingas, are just taking a sunbath, drying their feathers after a dip in the refreshing water.

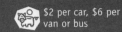
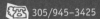

marauding wildlife, kids still have the opportunity to spot the ibis, osprey, cattle egret, great blue heron, and anhinga, as well as birds that hunt near the water such as the red-shoulder hawk. Owls also populate the park, and nightly "owl prowls" are sponsored during the winter.

Bike trails and challenging nature trails beckon, where watchful kids might encounter a variety of wildlife from cooters (a kind of turtle) to foxes. A coral rock boathouse has been converted into a concession stand that rents rowboats and paddleboats, which you can take out on the freshwater lagoon. For a more challenging course, set a canoe on the Oleta River, or book a tee time at the popular golf course on the other side of the park.

KEEP IN MIND
As with many of the area's parks, wear the right clothing when walking or biking. Make sure you and your kids are wearing closed-toe shoes. During the rainy season, its best to wear long-sleeve shirts and long pants, despite the heat, to protect yourself from the mosquitoes.

KID-FRIENDLY EATS
The park exits into an urban area filled with food choices. Nearby, you can sample Thai and Japanese food at **Thai House II Restaurant and Sushi Bar** (2250 N.E. 163rd St., tel. 305/940–6075), or you can keep going with the nature theme and stop at **Artichoke's Natural Cuisine** (3055 N.E. 163rd St., tel. 305/945–7576), where kids will find plenty of pasta and chicken dishes to their liking.

GULFSTREAM PARK FAMILY DAY

This horse-racing complex is more than just a place that takes bets on equines. Every Sunday during the season (November–March), Gulfstream sponsors family day, providing a number of activities designed to appeal to children of all ages, not to mention their folks. Toddlers may want to ride around the grassy ring on top of one of the ponies saddled for kids 2 and up. The ponies also range in size, allowing bigger kids 6 and up to saddle up without their feet hitting the ground.

Other activities include a petting zoo. Fancy chickens, box turtles, and a couple of rather disinterested goats shuffle slowly around a fenced-in pen, which is helpful in keeping both children and animals under control. The animals are used to being stroked, but parents are required to attend to their kids so no one is accidentally trampled by tiny feet. A few

HEY, KIDS!

The park can get pretty crowded, so if you want to ride the ponies, chances are you'll have to stand in line. Fortunately, everyone always gets a turn, and you don't have to worry about falling off. An attendant will lead the horse by the reins as you grip the saddle horn.

KEEP IN MIND

With each child, one adult gets in free. Add in the no-hassle, no-pay parking and you've got yourself a reasonably priced, event-filled day. The more popular acts draw plenty of fans, so keep an eye on your kids. Though you may want to avoid the grandstands, the cleanest bathrooms are inside the racing facility.

yards away from the petting zoo, a rock-climbing wall challenges kids age 8 and up. Like the ponies and zoo, the wall is supervised by trained professionals, who hook the kids up with carabiners and let them rappel down the wall after they've victoriously reached the top.

Teens, however, mostly come here to catch the classic rock-and-roll acts that play the park's amphitheater all winter long. The live weekend concerts, which are free with admission, attract a good crowd, and the amphitheater is set far away from the grandstands. In addition, the "seating" is basically a long grassy lawn that beckons beach towels, lawn chairs, and picnic baskets. At the best shows, it's not unusual to find a 50-year-old dancing next to a teenager, who in turn has a younger sibling by the hand. Even if the kids don't recognize the act, they might be familiar with the songs.

KID-FRIENDLY EATS Plenty of fast-food stands provide kids with all the foods they love the best—hot dogs, pizza, ice cream, and lemonade. You can enjoy a picnic while you watch the concert, but if you're planning to unpack on a square of grass to call your own, it's best to arrive early.

HAULOVER PARK BEACH AND MARINA

36

S wimming, boogie-boarding, people-watching, and many more activities are all part of a relaxing day at the beach. This 182-acre expanse of pristine white sand draws visitors from the world over. When you and your kids are lazing in the sun, keep a finely tuned ear over the intermittent crash of the sea. You're likely to hear conversations in French, Spanish, Creole, Italian, Portuguese, and the patois of many different islands.

Huddled between the Intracoastal Waterway and the Atlantic Ocean, this beach distinguishes itself in a variety of ways. The open surf provides spectacular waves, perfect for surfing and boogie-boarding. Highly trained lifeguards patrol the beach so parents can relax. The surf and good head wind allow kids to keep kites in the air longer than anywhere else in Miami. Roadside concession stands rent and/or sell a variety of fanciful kites. If you're a novice kite-flyer, ask the vendors for tips on getting the kites in the air, and make sure

KEEP IN MIND Sunstroke (also called heatstroke) is a very real possibility in Florida. Most physicians define sunstroke as overexposure to direct sun on a person who is unaccustomed to a hot climate. It's even more common in a humid climate like Miami's, where the body has reduced ability to cool itself. Watch for symptoms in yourself and your children—fatigue, weakness, and faintness. Keep in mind, too, that initially sunstroke brings on profuse sweating, but that more advanced sunstroke can lead to hot, dry skin and rapid elevation in temperature. If you think someone in your family has sunstroke, take him or her at once to the nearest emergency room.

10800 Collins Ave., Miami Beach

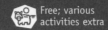 Free; various activities extra

 Daily 7–sunset

305/944–3040

 All ages

you buy a good one for beginners. Some of the kites available are so sophisticated they look like marionettes in the air, and kids may have trouble controlling them.

Shaded picnic areas, perfect for a brief respite from sun and fun, dot the beach. And for the budding anglers in the family, take the underground path to the other side of the street to visit Haulover Park Marina, which houses the largest drift fishing/charter fleet in the business. From here, kids with strong stomachs can sign on for a half day or full day of deep-sea fishing for yellowtail snapper and grouper, or simply drop a line off the jetty for snook, tarpon, and amberjack (only amberjack is a good eating fish). For another diversion, kids can check out the family-friendly 9-hole golf course, tennis courts, and the souvenir shop.

KID-FRIENDLY EATS The beach has picnic areas with grills and an assortment of concession stands, but even easier is a quick trip across the street to the marina for ultra-casual dockside dining. Somehow, eating fresh-cooked seafood always tastes better when it's served with a view of the water.

HEY, KIDS! Lifeguards are trained in everything from emergency rescue to underwater search and recovery. Many are even qualified as emergency technicians and paramedics. In addition, the Miami lifeguards keep visitors informed of dangerous water conditions. So if a lifeguard tells you not to go in the water or to come out immediately, do it.

HISTORICAL MUSEUM OF
SOUTHERN FLORIDA

This museum celebrates 10,000 years of Native American, Caribbean, Jewish, and Latin heritage with life-size, hands-on exhibits. After all, nowhere in Miami can children hear an entire symphony of jungle sounds, ranging from the deep bass of caiman roars to the piccolo trill of insects, stroll through the porch of a typical Florida house (without worrying about trespassing), and climb on a real-life trolley car from the turn-of-the-last century.

Begin your exploration at the permanent exhibit "Tropical Dreams." Kids 2 and up will especially enjoy the life-size diorama of indigenous peoples, the replica of a Spanish galleon, and the actual shipboard cannons, which are safe for kids to touch. Past shows have included "A Slave Ship Speaks," an exhibition of historical artifacts recovered from the oldest slave shipwreck, the *Henrietta Marie,* sunk near Key West in 1701.

From there, move on to the collections. Large first- and second-edition prints from John James Audubon's *The Birds of America* portray a variety of birds from the

HEY, KIDS!
The museum has documented the traditional arts of more than 60 cultural groups, all of which live in South Florida. See if you can find the Cuban yard shrine, the Haitian sign art, and the Venezuelan mask.

KID-FRIENDLY EATS The museum doesn't have a restaurant on premises, but it is right in the middle of downtown, so scoring a hot dog from a sidewalk vendor is great for a fast lunch. Sit-down options include the healthy-but-tasty **Granny Feelgood's** (25 W. Flagler St., tel. 305/377–9600) and Bayside Marketplace, where **Dick's Last Resort** (401 N.E. Biscayne Blvd., tel. 305/375–6575) and **Hard Rock Cafe** (401 N.E. Biscayne Blvd., tel. 305/377–3110) are constant kid-pleasers.

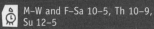

American flamingo to the scarlet ibis. Large-letter postcards (think letters as puffy as clouds spelling out "Miami") will captivate kids age 6 and up who are learning penmanship. The Miami Centennial Quilt, a handmade document of city life, depicts the history of Miami from the early part of the 20th century with 30 colorfully illustrated blocks, making kids wonder what a "Millennial" quilt would look like.

Conclude your visit with a bang—literally. The museum displays an extensive collection of Caribbean percussion instruments, such as the Cuban conga drum, the Trinidadian steel drum, and the Haitian Rada ensemble. Through sound bites, history, and explanation of how each instrument is used, the collection is a musical portrait of 10 island nations. Such a wide variety of sound machines makes most parents grateful that these joyfully noisy items are being stored in a museum—and not in their own houses.

KEEP IN MIND The Historical Museum store, the Indies Company, offers a terrific selection of books, jewelry, toys, and gifts related to Florida history and the exhibitions. Some are as educational as they are fun. Pop in here to give kids a break from the exhibits, even if you only intend to browse.

HOLOCAUST MEMORIAL

A sobering experience may not be everyone's ideal outing. And this memorial, honoring the 6 million Jews who died in the Holocaust, is moving, to say the least. Parents should first decide whether or not kids can handle the material, which is indeed disturbing. For the most part, teens will be the ones to get an education from this experience.

The complex has much to offer. A variety of sculptures rooted to the ground are all expressively, beautifully rendered. In particular, a woman with a shawl folded across her face is startlingly moving without being explicit. The names of the 28 concentration camps are chiseled in a tunnel that plays eerie music, and the names of the 6 million Jews are inscribed on nearly 100 standing slabs of black marble.

The centerpiece of the memorial is a 45-ft high bronze arm rising from a pond choked with lily pads. On the arm, tortured figures try to make their way to the fingers, which

KEEP IN MIND Like the American Police Hall of Fame & Museum, this site, even if toured by age-appropriate children, can be at best disturbing. Some kids might need quiet reflection afterward, others might need activity. If the latter is the case and your kids are old enough to play a few holes, consider the 18-hole golf course across the street on Alton Road—it's open to the public and easily accessible.

1933–1945 Meridian Ave., South Beach

 Free

 Daily 9–9

305/538–1663

 12 and up

represent escape. Some of the figures seem like they're about to fall, which can be profoundly upsetting. Indeed, the sculptures are astonishingly detailed, with facial features reflecting various hopes and agonies. The wrist itself is tattooed with a number, just like the wrists of German Jews in the concentration camps.

Fortunately, because of the circular route of the memorial, you can stop at any time and go back the way you came if the images become too pressing. Although the memorial has many sculptures and photos to examine, it's rather small. Directly behind the memorial is a small botanical garden, a sweet-smelling refuge to take your kids to air out opinions about the memorial. For serious relief, Lincoln Road bustles in all its commercial glory two blocks to the south. Ocean Drive is also only a bit to the east, where the only memorials are the ones set up to worship the sun.

HEY, KIDS! In a cartoon, a young man is climbing a huge mountain to visit a wise man. But when he gets there, all the wise man says is, "We're all different and we're all the same." What do you think he means?

KID-FRIENDLY EATS Lincoln Road's multitudinous sidewalk cafés are at hand just two blocks to the south. Check out **Paninoteca** (809 Lincoln Rd., tel. 305/538–0058) for scrumptious gourmet sandwiches or **Van Dyke Café** (846 Lincoln Rd., tel. 305/534–3600) for a pinch of people-watching and a dash of bistro fare.

HOMESTEAD-MIAMI SPEEDWAY

The smell of burning rubber. The roar of powerful engines. The race cars and jump-suited crew emblazoned with patches from sponsors. Ready, set, go! For the kids who love loud noises and fast cars, this racetrack is a thrilling adventure. Some of the biggest races in the country are held here: the NASCAR Winston Cup, the Miami 300 NASCAR Busch Series, and the Pennzoil 400. Parents might cringe, but kids will thrill to see race cars cornering the 1.5-mi track at speeds upward of 125 mi per hour. It's a far cry from playing pretend with matchbox cars.

Expanded in 1999, the 434-acre complex now seats 72,000. Grandstands flank the speedway, and there are concessions outside the grandstands but inside the gates. Kids will appreciate the informative programs, so they'll know when a speedway record is being challenged. The Speedway already has record holders, such as Michael Andretti, who holds

HEY, KIDS!

The Miami Grand Prix, one of Miami's biggest and most challenging races, doesn't even take place at the Speedway. Every March, Downtown Miami is barricaded from regular traffic so drivers can race through the city.

KEEP IN MIND
The big races stretch out over weekends and attract a national fan base. As a result, area hotels and restaurants can get very crowded, not to mention the Speedway itself. Young children under 6 can easily get lost; it's best not to bring them at all. They also might be frightened by the loud noises and pressing crowds. Keep other children close by, and for safety reasons, don't sit too near the track.

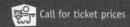
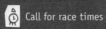

the track record for continuous highest speed during a race (144.339 mi per hour). The speedway announcer will be sure to let you know when a record is broken. Races can be even more exciting when kids can root for something specific.

But it's not only cars that speed around the speedway's oval cement track. NASCAR's most competitive race is the 1999 Craftsman Truck Series. It's one thing to see low-slung cars gliding swiftly around the track, and quite another to watch pickup trucks lumber around the track at top speeds. As with the cars, returning champions such as Jack Sprague, Greg Biffle, and Mike Wallace are usually on hand, either to defend their titles or at least to sign autographs—another good reason to buy a program. Make sure your kids have a pen or pencil handy!

KID-FRIENDLY EATS You can count on **Main Street Café** (128 N. Krome Ave., tel. 305/245–7099) for a wholesome meal for the entire family. For breakfast any time, the **International House of Pancakes** (399 S. Homestead Blvd., tel. 305/248–1990) always appeals.

INTERNATIONAL GAME FISH ASSOCIATION HALL OF FAME & MUSEUM

J ust over the Miami-Dade county line, the IGFA Hall of Fame & Museum surprises both anglers and nonanglers with facts about fish. Upon entering, your kids get a fish-eye's view of the world by looking up at the ceiling, which is constructed to resemble the bottom of the hull of a wooden boat. The silver tiles on the walls represent fish scales, and silver fish "swim" through the air. Even the floor has been colored to resemble the sand at the bottom of the ocean. A soundtrack plays seabirds calls, the rush of wind, and the crash of waves.

Once inside, the lobby leads directly into the Fishing Hall of Fame, where an impressive 172 real fish dangle from the ceiling. All are record-holding trophy fish, which have been donated to the museum by the lucky anglers who caught them. Plaques under the fish commemorate the record holders, give information about the fish, and other specifics. Children's jaws will fall to the floor upon inspecting the monstrous 2,664-pound great white shark and the 35-pound barracuda.

HEY, KIDS! Before a catch can become a record, its size and weight must be estimated by sight. If it looks like a possible record-breaker, the angler tries to land it. If he or she succeeds, the fish must be weighed by a weighmaster, or an IGFA official, and pictures must be taken of the fish, the angler, the tackle (the rod and reel), and the scale. Finally, the angler has to submit an official application. Sounds like a lot of work, but the hardest part is actually catching the fish!

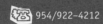
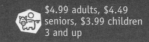
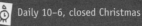

Other activities include the Fish Gallery, where kids can learn about habitats and conservation of various kinds of fish. The Marina, which floats on a 6-ft-deep lake, is stocked with largemouth bass, peacock bass, catfish, and long-ear sunfish (for a quarter, you can buy fish food and toss it into the lake). For a virtual experience, check out the fishing games in the Catch Gallery, where kids as young as 4 can land a fish.

In the Bait and Tackle Shop, an ingenuous tribute to old-time fishermen, park your youngest in the Junior Anglers room or the Discovery Room, where 2–7-year-olds can wear fishing vests, catch "fish" from a play boat, and make fish prints. Finally, finish up with a stroll through the 4-acre Wetlands via the 730-ft elevated boardwalk. Underneath your feet, 45 species of birds, brown basilisk lizards, moorhens, harlequin ducks, turtles, and even baby alligators congregate in the swamp. Numerous food machines along the way allow children to entice the wildlife a little closer with the promise of something good to eat.

KID-FRIENDLY EATS A **Subway Café** inside the museum is a quick pit stop for a sandwich, a slice of pizza, and a drink. But if you walk across the parking lot to the **Islamorada Fish Company** (200 Gulf Stream Way, tel. 954/927–7737), a fresh fish sandwich—or even a burger and fries—in this well-known eatery is bound to satisfy.

KEEP IN MIND All areas containing water are carefully fenced off, so kids, especially toddlers, are not in any danger of getting their feet wet. Avoid resting a small child on top of the metal barriers that protect the ponds and the wooden fences that surround the wetlands. Though tots can certainly get a better view of the fish and wildlife this way, they can also fall in. Even if they don't fall, you're teaching them a lesson that could prove dangerous in other settings, such as in zoos and on balconies.

JACKIE GLEASON THEATRE OF
PERFORMING ARTS

S trolling through the spacious lobby of this elegant and popular theater is a bit like stepping into a time warp. Once a center for Miami Beach social gatherings, with its soaring ceilings and glittering chandeliers, it now stages a variety of productions that promise to entertain both children and parents.

In one week, you might see world champion ballroom dancers do the tango, hear a sitar performance by Ravi Shankar, or be enchanted by a Miami City Ballet matinee. Broadway musicals, performed by professional touring companies, range from *Rent* to *Blood Brothers*, which children over the age of 12 will appreciate. Younger children will be dazzled by shows such as Blues' Clues Live and fairy-tale adaptations of *Beauty and the Beast* and *The Lion King*. The theater also hosts a variety of concerts, primarily because of its dynamic acoustics. Past performers have included Tori Amos and Crosby, Stills & Nash.

HEY, KIDS!
Jackie Gleason was an extremely popular comedian in the 1950s. His most famous role was that of Ralph Kramden on the now-classic show *The Honeymooners*, which was one of the first successful television sitcoms.

KEEP IN MIND Avoid the valet parking; instead, take advantage of the pay parking lots across the street. Be careful not to park in residential neighborhoods, however tempting it may be. Many of these spaces are designated for residents and require permits.

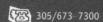
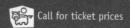
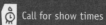

The theater was originally named the Miami Beach Auditorium and was well known for hosting the *Jackie Gleason Show* during the 1960s. After Gleason passed away in 1987, it was renamed in his honor. In 1992, the theater underwent an extensive renovation and now seats about 2,700 people in both orchestra and mezzanine seating. There really isn't a bad seat in the house.

Though pantsuits on women or even jeans on men are perfectly acceptable attire, most folks like to dress up when they attend the theater here. It's one of the few places in ultracasual South Florida where women can deck themselves out in the gowns from their closets and men wear ties and jackets. It's best to arrive a half hour prior to performances. For performance listings, see the *Miami Herald* weekend section.

KID-FRIENDLY EATS Lincoln Road is only steps away from the theater. After the show sit at **Spris** (731 Lincoln Rd., tel. 305/673–2020), where you can choose from more than 30 different kinds of thin-crust pizza.

JOHN PENNECAMP CORAL REEF STATE PARK

This incredible aquatic world, with its tunnels, turrets, and towers, will thrill children of all ages. The first underwater preserve in the United States, Pennecamp includes 78 mi of living coral reef, which is made up of more than 50 different kinds of the corals and is home to more than 650 species of fish. The colorful interactions between reef and tropical fish are as breathtaking as any rainbow, and even better, because you don't have to wait for a rainy day to see it. Plus, if you've ever wanted to teach your kids to snorkel, this underwater park is the place to do it.

It takes a good 30 minutes to get to the reef by boat, and only about 30 seconds for curious kids to want to slip into the warm water and explore. Fortunately, the boat crew provides a 15-minute lesson for beginners, so parents can feel comfortable doing some snorkeling themselves. The whole excursion, which takes a little less than three hours,

HEY, KIDS! One of the reasons this park attracts so many fish and assorted aquatic life is because the staff works hard to keep the water clean. Remember if you have something to throw away, wait until you're back at the visitor center, where there are plenty of garbage cans.

Mile Marker 102.5, Key Largo

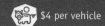 $4 per vehicle

  Daily 8–5

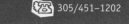 305/451–1202

All ages

costs $23.95 for adults and $18.95 for children and includes mask, flippers, life vest, and snorkel rental. Departure times are at 9, noon, and 3.

Divers should be on the lookout for a famous underwater statue called the "Christ of the Deep," which is at Dry Rocks. For toddlers and other children who haven't quite grown into flippers or wet suits yet, glass-bottom boat tours are an excellent option. In the visitor center, a 30,000-gallon saltwater aquarium provides aquatic entertainment for the land-bound, and touch-tanks allow youngsters of all ages to get friendly with turtles and other marine life. For family outings, try renting a canoe, sailboat, or motorboat, and do a little fishing along the way. You can cook your catch at any of the 47 campsites, provided you've made a reservation.

KID-FRIENDLY EATS Key Largo is loaded with fast-food options. If you're looking for a relaxing, sit-down dinner after a long day in the water, hustle your kids to the **Crack'd Conch** (Mile Marker 105, tel. 305/451–0732), where they can munch on conch fritters and you can sip one of the 100 different kinds of beer.

KEEP IN MIND The camp is a popular day trip from Miami. Schools plan frequent field trips here, so reservations for snorkeling and glass-bottom boat tours are essential. If you're planning on camping, don't forget the essential bug repellent. The mosquitoes can be awfully fierce, especially during the summer months.

KENDALL INDIAN HAMMOCKS PARK

I f you like golf but find it a little on the slow side—all that walking in between the few times you get to whack the ball with a club—perhaps tossing around a Frisbee is an option. But if you don't have enough kids to get together a good game of Ultimate, what can you play? Easy. Try your hand—and throwing arm—at disc golf.

The object of this unusual sport is simple: fling a Frisbee at a "hole," which is really a chain-link basket 3 ft in diameter, and hope it goes in, or at least near, the basket. Score is kept the same as golf. As in regular golf, distances from the tees to the holes vary, and some can be about 400 yards, so chances are you'll be making lots of stops along the way. You can spend as long as four hours on a single round. In general, the pace of disc golf seems a little sprightlier, with less stuffy rules, than regular golf. And you can make

HEY, KIDS!
The trick to throwing a Frisbee is in the wrist. If you can make your wrist snap forward as you release the disc, chances are you'll get a smooth flight. A firm grip and good timing also help you reach your target. Don't worry if you don't get the hang of it right away. Practice makes perfect.

KEEP IN MIND
Many of the parks are particularly crowded on weekends, which can be stimulating for the children but also frustrating if you intend on spending quality family time. Weekday mornings are the quietest times for visiting parks; they tend to fill up when school is over for the day.

a round go faster by jogging to your Frisbee. South Florida is home to four disc golf courses. This particular course, spread out over grassy open meadows spiked with large shade trees, is the only one to have 18 official holes—the other three have 9 holes each.

Aside from the disc golf option, the park caters to preschool neighborhood children. Plenty of birthday parties are celebrated here under the chickee hut, a replica of an Indian dwelling. Set in the trees, a platform is an ideal place to picnic. But it's the play area that receives the undivided attention from the too-young-to-golf set. Wooden jungle gyms include a challenging rope bridge, a tire swing, and several different shapes of slides. The good news, too, is that the disc golf course is far enough away so that you don't have to worry about stray Frisbees sailing into the heads of the youngest kids.

KID-FRIENDLY EATS Plenty of chain and fast-food restaurants dot this suburban area. For something a little more stimulating, head over to North Kendall Drive. You can sample everything from Chinese food at **Chifa** (12590 N. Kendall Dr., tel. 305/271–3823) and Indian fare at **Punjab Palace** (11780 N. Kendall Dr., tel. 305/386–0545) to **Romano's Macaroni Grill** (12100 N. Kendall Dr., tel. 305/270–0621).

LARRY & PENNY THOMPSON PARK
AND CAMPGROUND

Despite the plethora of parks, Miami is at times so urban that it's hard to recall days of yore, which really weren't all that long ago. So for the sake of history, and the pleasure of giving your school-age kids a good story to tell their friends, try sleeping outdoors in January. This park and campground combines comforts of home—electrical and water hookups, four large rest room/laundry facilities with hot showers, a camp store, picnic shelters, and cookout facilities for each campsite—with all the benefits of nature.

Aside from the amenities, the park offers a welcome respite from bustling Miami. Kids will love the freshwater lake, which is stocked with fat bass ripe for plucking from the water, and the twisting, winding water slide, which is a sneaky way to get dirty offspring clean. Nature trails are ideal for a challenging run or mountain-biking. Athletic teens may even

HEY, KIDS! Don't pick up stray mangoes with your hands. You may be allergic to the sap and skin and will develop a rash after touching them. People who pick mangoes from the trees wear protective gloves. However, don't lose an opportunity to try a mango. The most popular fruit in the world, mangoes taste like a cross between two fruits. The first one is a peach. Try and guess the other.

12451 S.W. 184 St., South Miami-Dade

 305/232-1049

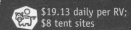 $19.13 daily per RV; $8 tent sites

 Daily 8–6

 All ages

take to the 20-station fitness course, which is something like an obstacle course designed to work up developing muscles.

The fruit trees are perhaps the most striking part of the park. Mango, litchi, and avocado trees act as wind buffers for the campsites, and you can often hear fruit dropping from them at night. Native palmettos and rock pinelands may be expected, but the seasonal displays of wildflowers are always a treat. And if you're very quiet at night, you might hear the roar of a tiger or chatter of a monkey carrying over from the MetroZoo, adjacent to the park. Add in a couple of owl hoots and parrot squawks, and kids will really feel like they're camping in a jungle.

KID-FRIENDLY EATS Although the park has a concession stand, most campers enjoy bringing and cooking their own burgers, dogs, and of course, marshmallows. Try the last paired with fresh mangoes for a juicy, sticky sweet.

KEEP IN MIND The camp makes a great overnight trip when combined with the MetroZoo and the Gold Coast Railroad Museum. The campground can get crowded, so be sure to make reservations in advance.

LINCOLN ROAD WALKING MALL

One of the hottest spots in Miami, Lincoln Road is ideal for the entire family. For toddlers, the expansive, car-free walking mall is stroller-friendly (and conducive for running). For kids 6 and up, it's Rollerblade central, though crowds of pedestrians can make it something of an obstacle course. And for teens, it's the perfect people-watching thoroughfare on the way to the beach.

Actually, Lincoln Road has changed quite a bit since the 1950s, when it was anchored by major department stores. In the 1970s and '80s, it fell into a tremendous decline and was virtually abandoned. Then, at the beginning of the South Beach Renaissance, local artists and various Bohemian types found the rents cheap enough and the spaces conducive for studios, a few pioneering restaurants, and plenty of eclectic boutiques. The mall became an artsy hangout, populated by residents but of not much interest to visitors.

HEY, KIDS!
Keep your eyes peeled for celebrities. Cameron Diaz owns a restaurant on one of the side streets that intersect the mall. George Clooney, Matt Dillon, and Rupert Everett all like to hang out in Miami, too.

Today, thanks to landscaping, sparkling fountains, art deco sculptures, and zillions of successful sidewalk cafés, the mall is a premier attraction. Trendy clothing shops line

KID-FRIENDLY EATS Because most of the many cafés have both inside and outside seating, almost all of them are kid friendly. Of particular interest is **Balans** (1022 Lincoln Rd., tel. 305/534–9191), a British-influenced eatery that serves daily breakfast and weekend brunch. For real Miami eats, check out Cuban joints **Lincoln Road Café** (941 Lincoln Rd., tel. 305/538–8066) and **David's Café II** (1654 Meridian Ave., tel. 305/672–8707).

Free

Lincoln Rd., between Washington Ave. and West Ave., South Beach

 n/a

 All ages

n/a

the road, as well as pop artist Romero Britto's storefront and the maze of working studios that comprise the South Florida Arts Center. At night, many of the cafés hire musicians, plus plenty of itinerants set up in doorways. Thus the music on the road is quite literal, mostly percussion and Spanish guitar.

Perch anywhere for some of the best people-watching in Miami. Models flip through their portfolios while waiting for calls from their agents, and businessfolk conduct their affairs via cell phone while they relax in the sun. The local TV station WAMI broadcasts from the Sony Building on Lincoln Road, and catalog photos for stores like Filene's Basement and scenes for movies (such as *There's Something About Mary* and *Ace Ventura: Pet Detective*) are often shot here as well. So be sure to smile as you trip over the sound equipment wires—you never know when that camera will be candid.

KEEP IN MIND On Saturday and Sunday during the winter season, Lincoln Road hosts several events, including a crafts-and-collectibles fair and a farmers' market. These daylong festivities can be quite entertaining but are often crowded, and parking can be a hassle. It's best to arrive early, which on Lincoln Road means about 10 AM.

LOWE ART MUSEUM

At this museum, kids will discover the tools of everyday life from ancient times. This spacious, circuitous museum houses some of the most important collections in South Florida. Its rich and varied collection of more than 10,000 pieces includes a pre-Colombian assortment of tools and weapons and a plethora of Egyptian, Greek, and Roman antiquities, such as cups from Greece dating from 565 BC and masks from Rome dating from mid-2nd century AD.

The Lowe's mission is one of cultural and ethnic diversity, a statement that's continually borne out by its extracurricular activities. Children will benefit from many of these activities, such as Kids' Day: Medieval and Renaissance Women in which, in honor of Mother's Day, kids explore the depiction of women in the Medieval and Renaissance collection and paint their own images during the studio activity that follows. It sounds esoteric, but the end result is where kids have the most fun. The museum also frequently hosts classical concerts such as the Ravel and Debussy movement series and poetry readings by renowned

HEY, KIDS! After you're done touring the museum, take a look around the University of Miami. You'll see plenty of students bustling around with backpacks on their way to class or lying around under palm trees with their friends. UM is well known for its champion football and baseball teams, and while the football stadium (the Orange Bowl) is located in Miami, the Mark Light baseball stadium is on the campus. In 1999, the Canes won the College World Series, and some of the players have gone on to the big leagues.

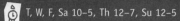

Cuban poet and art critic Ricardo Pau-Llosa. These events can seem a little odd when they're posed against a backdrop of a temporary exhibit like the Big Apple paintings and drawing that comprise "Manhattan Stories." But in a way, the diversity of the museum reflects the city's character.

Most of the individual collections can be traced back to the interest of a benefactor. For example, the outstanding Native American collection began in 1956 with a donation by Alfred I. Barton; the Samuel H. Kress Foundation granted the museum an enormous collection of Renaissance and Baroque paintings; and winter resident Stephen Junkunc started the museum's Asian collection with an astounding assortment of Chinese, Korean, and Japanese ceramics, paintings, and sculptures. None of this will mean much to kids, but it's interesting for parents to explain just how all this art came to be housed under one roof.

KEEP IN MIND

Since this museum is on a college campus, parking is tough. Your best bet is to use the museum lot, which has metered parking. Fortunately, the Lowe is near the central entrance to UM, so it's relatively easy to find. Just ask the guard at the main gate to point the way. For a keepsake, visit the museum store for gifts, jewelry, and reproductions of artwork.

KID-FRIENDLY EATS
Not much is available to nonstudent or nonfaculty. A homey little pub right at the edge of campus, **Titanic Brewing Company** (5813 Ponce de Leon Blvd., tel. 305/667–2537) is more of a restaurant than a bar (at least during the day). A half mile away, the funky **Fishbone Grille** (1450 S. Dixie Hwy., tel. 305/668–3033) offers great, innovative seafood at reasonable prices.

MATHESON HAMMOCK BEACH
PARK AND MARINA

This park stands out for its man-made atoll pool, a wide and shallow lagoon that's perfect for little ones who are either learning to swim or just want to frolic about. The pool is flushed naturally with the tidal waters of Biscayne Bay, and the bathtub-warm temperatures are the result of a combination of shallow water and strong sun.

On the right side of the park, past the tollgate, splendid saltwater fishing prospects abound. The best spots for snapper, mullet, and snook are under the bridge, where it's relatively quiet. Be prepared to get wet, though, and hold on tight to children with poor balance. The 100-acre park was recovered from a mangrove swamp, and the mangrove roots spread everywhere and are easy to trip over. For a closer look at these trees with limbs that twist as if they'd been in a hurricane (many of them have), take a half-hour hike along the nature path through the mangroves.

KEEP IN MIND Rest rooms and showers are conveniently located, so you don't have to bring the beach back home with you. Because the park seems to have as much soil as sand, kids can get awfully dirty fast, so do take advantage of the facilities.

KID-FRIENDLY EATS The ever-popular concession stands dish out the children-pleasing hot dogs and hamburgers. But if your kids are durable enough, hang out 'til sunset and eat at the Red Fish Grill (tel. 305/668–8788), a fine-dining restaurant serving inventive American fare, in one of the historic coral buildings. Outdoor seating is available, and offers nightly colorfully lit views of Downtown Miami and Miami Beach.

Built in the 1930s on land donated by pioneer and conservationist Commodore J. W. Matheson, this park is the oldest in Miami. However, most of the current action has to do with the here-and-now of teenager's lives. In addition to the baby friendliness of the pool and beach, local kids of all ages hang out here during school vacations and summers. It can get crowded, so arrive early for a prime spot to spread the beach blanket.

When the sun goes down, look at the Miami skyline. More than 40 skyscrapers have different lighting patterns, and together they resemble a brilliant Christmas-like display. Vibrant, colorful lights even adorn the tracks of the Metromover, an elevated train that runs around downtown, and the numerous bridges connecting the mainland to the beaches.

HEY, KIDS! Due to overfishing in certain areas, some of Miami's local sport fish, such as swordfish and sea bass, are now endangered. You can do your part in conservation by throwing back undersize fish, which have not reached the reproductive age. Check with bait-and-tackle shops to find out the legal limits for the fish you are likely to hook.

MIAMI ART MUSEUM

Miami is sometimes known as the crossroads of the Americas, and Miami Art Museum's (MAM) mission is "to collect, preserve and interpret international art with a focus on the art of the Western Hemisphere from the World War II era to the present." The museum displays exhibits from the 1940s onward, devoting itself to collections stemming from North, Central, and South America, including the Caribbean, and occasionally presenting work from a previous era to provide some historical perspective.

Most likely, depending on when you visit, you'll encounter familiar images from Andy Warhol to William Wegman. These pop pieces and whimsical photographs are especially entertaining for children, who will be awed at how these artists interpreted everyday objects such as soup cans and pet dogs. You can ask kids to identify shapes—circles, triangles, and so on—in the pictures and match them to a preprinted guidebook available at the museum. Older kids will appreciate MAM's attempt to involve the rest of the artistic community—

KEEP IN MIND The Miami Art Museum is adjacent to the Historical Museum of Southern Florida, and lies directly across from the Main Public Library, which houses art exhibits in the auditorium and second-floor library. These three buildings make up what's known as the 3-acre Metro-Dade Cultural Center. But touring the triad can be especially overwhelming for kids under 12.

 101 W. Flagler St.,
Downtown Miami

 305/375–1700

 $5 adults, $2.50 students/seniors, children under 12 free

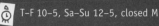 T–F 10–5, Sa–Su 12–5, closed M

 All ages

writers, musicians, and the like—with the exhibits. In the past, the museum has arranged shows featuring the works of several artists accompanied by related poems and stories penned by local authors. In this setting, you'll see the works in a new, interpretative light.

Most of the artistic mediums are represented through oil and watercolor paintings, line or pen-and-ink drawings, and lithographs and prints. Videos of artists at work can make the viewing experience more interactive, which while showing children the process as the product also teaches art appreciation. Annually, MAM hangs the Miami-Dade County Public Schools Scholastic Art Awards Exhibition, always of interest to both students and parents, whether they're locals who have participated or just curious visitors. Talent, as it turns out, doesn't age-discriminate.

HEY, KIDS! Try your hand at some art—the museum allows sketching from anywhere in the building. Take along a pad and several sharp pencils with you, then settle yourself in front of a painting you like and try to copy it. It doesn't have to be exactly like the original; it will be you're own interpretation.

KID-FRIENDLY EATS If you're not inclined to pack your own lunch, you can purchase crepes from one of the vendors that frequent the courthouse area (across the street on the south side of the Metro-Dade Cultural Center). Or try the **Royal Palm Café** (22 E. Flagler St., tel. 305/577–2420), the department store dining room of Burdine's, a major South Florida shopping mecca for subtropical fashions. Homemade fare includes potpie and jerk chicken.

MIAMI CITY BALLET

Without a doubt, the Miami City Ballet is one of the city's highlights for children who enjoy the drama of formal dance. Stirring music, colorful costumes, and whirling dancers are all ideal for holding a child's gaze captive, even if said kid is too young to understand the intricacies of the ballet.

The theater company focuses on the future of dance and on educating children of all ages through both performances and classes. Sunday-afternoon matinees are often geared toward children, and are sometimes even preceded by brunches or followed by tea parties. These light meals cost extra, but allow children to meet the ballet's founder and some of its dancers.

Artistic director Edward Villella, the first American-born male principal of the New York City Ballet, founded the ballet in 1985. Under his direction, the company specializes in the numerous masterworks of George Balanchine, plus the neoclassical work of resident choreographer Jimmy Gamonet De Los Heros. Some of the pieces contain adult themes, so parents should examine the material before purchasing tickets.

KID-FRIENDLY EATS Miami's Latin American dining scene includes a number of Colombian restaurants. One of the most reliable is **Mama Vieja** (239 23rd St., tel. 305/538–2400), where you can sample ceviche (marinated fish) and a variety of soups.

HEY, KIDS! During *The Nutcracker* season, the dancers will go through 725 pairs of toe shoes. Each show requires about 100 pounds of fake snow for the stage set, and each costume needs 2,500 yards of fabric. And just in case you were wondering, the cannon that is fired on stage uses real gunpowder for an effective *boom!*

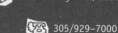 2200 Liberty Ave., South Beach

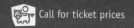 Call for ticket prices

 Call for show times and venues

305/929-7000

5 and up

Villella's wife, Linda, a professional figure skater, opened the Miami City Ballet School in January 1993 to train children for a lifelong career in ballet. Don't let the serious sound of that statement dissuade children who simply want to learn ballet for fun or self-improvement. The community classes offered teach children age 5 and up the basic steps, rhythm, and movement. Every year, the ballet performs the *Nutcracker* during the holiday season, with roles filled by children from the Ballet School.

The troupe used to rehearse in a small building on Lincoln Road, but has recently moved into a brand-new, state-of-the-art complex adjacent to the Bass Museum of Art. Thanks to the expanded space, the Ballet School can take in more students, some of whom will be groomed to dance in the company. The building has retained one feature from the cramped Lincoln Road location—storefront windows that allow passersby to watch exercises and studio rehearsals.

KEEP IN MIND The Miami City Ballet actually has three performance venues, one in each of three South Florida counties (Miami-Dade, Broward, and Palm Beach). In Miami, the company performs at the Jackie Gleason Theatre of Performing Arts. If you want to see more than one performance, you can purchase subscriptions to several concerts at the beginning of the season, which lasts from October until March.

MIAMI ICE ARENA

How do you spell relief from Miami's balmy 80°F winters and its sweltering 90°F-plus summers? I-c-e s-k-a-t-i-n-g in a city where summer never ends.

The indoor rink's temperatures are kept at chilly levels in order to keep the ice in skating shape. Although the brisk air will sooth sun-tired kids, it's a good idea to bring jackets or sweaters because the contrast from street to ice can be quite marked. In fact, this is the only place in Miami where kids can say they needed to wear a hat and mittens!

If your kids are from warm-weather climates, they may be ice-skating novices. Fortunately, ice-skating is much like Rollerblading in terms of balance. Kids need to steady themselves first in a standing position, then push forward slowly on one foot. Ice-skating blades are a bit trickier to handle than the rubber wheels on Rollerblades, though, because the ice is more slippery than concrete. Plus, the surface of an ice-skating blade is less than that

HEY, KIDS! A Zamboni might sound like some strange kind of noodle. But it's really the big machine that cleans the ice by melting the surface just a little. The steam-cleaning allows ridges and cuts, made by your skates, to be smoothed away, so there'll be smooth skating in your future.

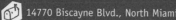 14770 Biscayne Blvd., North Miami

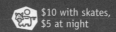 $10 with skates,
$5 at night

 Daily 11–2; T, W, and F nights 7:30–10

305/940–8222

 3 and up

of a Rollerblade, requiring greater control. The best advice for kids is to take it easy at first until they get the feel of the ice under their blades. Remember, falling on ice can be just as painful as falling on concrete. Remind kids who are used to fancy skating on Rollerblades to be more careful on ice skates because tricks, jumps, and turns are quite different on skates.

Don't worry about bringing skates along. The arena has plenty available for rental, and you can also lease a locker for your personal belongings. For nonskaters, a busy game room provides plenty of virtual action, including video basketball and martial arts games. Community hockey teams practice here, so it's wise to call ahead and make sure the ice is available for "all skate," which is when everyone is allowed to skate.

KEEP IN MIND

Kids in Miami may not be as used to skating on ice as they are on the street. So your kids are bound to have some bumps and bruises by the end of the excursion. What's the best way to treat swelling? Put ice on it, of course.

KID-FRIENDLY EATS The French-influenced **Gourmet Diner** (13951 Biscayne Blvd., tel. 305/947–2255) is one of the tastiest eateries in the city. Kids will love the stainless steel, truck-stop-diner decor, not to mention the skinny *pommes frites*, and parents will go for any of the reasonably priced entrées, including salmon or skirt steak.

MIAMI METROZOO

Two things Miami has plenty of—land and (mostly) good weather. The combination of these two virtues make this an ideal place for a zoo—and not just any zoo, but a cageless, free-range kind of zoo, where animals roam acres that have been designed to mimic their natural habitats. Some exhibits will resemble grass plains, others jungle forests. Moats, rather than wire cages, separate the 700 types of animals, ranging from gazelles and ostrich to kangaroos and wallabies, from people (and each other).

To get an overview of the entire zoo, start on the Zoofari monorail. The trip takes about 25 minutes and allows a pelican's-eye view of the exhibits. Children of all ages find the height a thrill in itself. Then, depending on your point of view, you can get off at Station 4 and make your way back to the entrance; or start at Station 1, the beginning, and stroll to Station 4. The zoo is laid out in a loose circle, with paved paths and exhibits on both sides, so in the end it all depends whether you like to work backward or forward.

HEY, KIDS!

Zoos don't only display animals, they also protect them from becoming extinct. Metro-Zoo breeds endangered animals such as crocodiles, African black rhinoceroses, elephants, and warthogs. When babies are born, the zoo allows them several months of privacy to grow and thrive before putting them on display.

KEEP IN MIND

Young children will get especially tired and cranky if you intend to see the entire zoo, which can easily take half a day. Give them frequent breaks at any of the playground areas, air-conditioned souvenir/gift shops, or picnic areas. You can also duck into the darkened viewing caves like the bat cave for respite from the sun. If you want to see the animals at their most active, plan to visit early in the morning or late in the afternoon, when the animals are post-nap and pre-feeding.

12400 S.W. 152 St., South Miami-Dade

 $8 adults, $4 children 3–12

 Daily 9:30–5:30

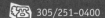 305/251-0400

 All ages

The zoo's 285 developed subtropical acres (out of a total of 740 acres) contain a huge range of animals, including gorillas, giraffes, and flamingos. Tiger Temple has been designed in keeping with the fabulous Asian River Life exhibit, and resembles the ruins of temple Angkor Wat, a site of religious pilgrimages, in Cambodia. As for Asian River Life, the exhibit contains clouded leopards, water monitors, and Komodo dragons, and visitors are treated to waterfalls, tropical mists, and exotic sounds as they examine the rare mammals and reptiles. Given the zoo's length and lack of shade, especially during midday, the Asian River Life exhibit is not only educational but cooling.

MetroZoo has two shows to entertain children: the Ecology Theater, which describes Florida's native wildlife, and the Wildlife Show, which presents an interesting variety of birds of prey such as ospreys and hawks, plus iguanas, snakes, and small mammals. PAWS, the petting zoo area, is also great fun for the younger kids, especially if they don't mind coming tummy-to-tummy with a potbellied pig.

KID-FRIENDLY EATS Restaurants and fast-food stands are scattered throughout the complex; hot dogs, hamburgers, and chicken sandwiches are the primary food focus, along with snacks such as popcorn and ice cream. You can also bring a picnic with you. A few kangaroo hops away, **J.R.'s Family Grill** (13744 S.W. 152nd St., tel. 305/233–8989) dishes up homemade dishes such as a hearty beef stew and cornflake-coated fried chicken.

MIAMI MUSEUM OF SCIENCE & SPACE
TRANSIT PLANETARIUM

Face down a giant, robotic Woolly Mammoth. Ride along with eagles, vultures, and other birds of prey. Separate fact from fantasy when it comes to sharks. At this museum and planetarium, science is anything but hands-off, and it's not limited to test tubes, chemicals, and stargazing. In fact, the 50-year-old museum's motto is "Making Science Fun." But the museum is dedicated to its community as well as its science projects, as demonstrated by its feature exhibit Smithsonian Expeditions: Exploring Latin America & the Caribbean. Since 1999 the institutions have jointly created the nation's first international science center called the Science Center of the Americas, which will prove a role model for science institutions all over the country.

The museum provides access to traveling exhibits, such as Skycycles, where children age 8 and up can test their high-wire ability, and marionette dinosaurs which they control. For more activity, check out the rock wall or challenge NBA players to a game of virtual

KEEP IN MIND The museum is ranked number one in the state against all other science, history, botanical, and zoological institutions, and was the first science museum nationwide to become an Upward Bound Math & Science Center. The museum is undergoing renovations, though, so call first to make sure the exhibits are open. If you're going to be in Miami for a while and think you might visit more than once, consider becoming a member—a family can join for $55, which is just about how much you'd pay for two visits.

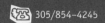
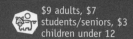
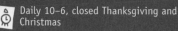

basketball. Kids will marvel at shows such as the Florida Marine Aquarium, with its colorful array of tropical fish and live coral, and the Wildlife Center, which is home to more than 175 reptiles. Also of interest is the Falcon Bachelor Bird of Prey Center, where injured birds of prey are rehabilitated before being released back into the wild.

Admission includes the planetarium, so don't miss out on the hourly shows explaining the stars and planets. Friday and Saturday night laser shows such as Laser Metallica 2000 and Pink Floyd Dark Side of the Moon cost extra to attend, but they're a great scene for teens who don't get easily motion sick. A modern rock show is especially popular, so call ahead for ticket prices and be prepared to stand in line.

HEY, KIDS! If you've never pet an iguana, here's your chance. You'll be surprised how this dry, bumpy reptile responds to being touched—it likes the warmth of your hands. After you leave the museum, watch the trees for other specimens. Iguanas are not uncommon in the South Florida wild, but you'll need to keep a sharp eye out for them to find them in all the camouflage.

KID-FRIENDLY EATS Snack machines and a hot dog vendor are on the premises, along with picnic tables. But you can get an entire meal just as quickly a mile or two down the road at the **Daily Bread Marketplace** (2400 S.W. 26th St., tel. 305/856–5893), a self-service Middle-Eastern café, grocery store, and bakery. Even if the kids don't want falafel, they're bound to fall for the honey-rich baklava.

MIAMI SEAQUARIUM

Lately, this 40-year-old theme park has seemed more shabby than sharp, but there's not a kid who doesn't love watching Lolita, a 10,000-pound killer whale, fling herself into the air. Those age 2 and up marvel at this 20-ft-long whale, who's capable of drenching the first 10 rows of the stadium seats in a single bound. Indeed, her show is perfect entertainment for a hot summer's day, as are the Top Deck Dolphin, Golden Dome Sea Lion, and shark shows. You can even plan your day around it, since Lolita performs at 11:45 AM and 3:40 PM.

The rain forest, wildlife habitat, and crocodile pit are good places for photo opportunities, though perhaps not quite as good as your children's faces when they see two sea lions kissing. A marine-life pool houses anything from a sea turtle to a stingray, none of which bite but may startle youngsters. A playground inside the gates is a perfect oasis for toddlers.

The Seaquarium is also known for several other famous marine animals, including Flipper the dolphin. Note, however, that while babies and toddlers will enjoy these shows, not all performance pools are stroller-friendly. Bring a stroller that will easily fold up

HEY, KIDS!
The manatee is a marine mammal—not a fish—that grows up to 1,000 pounds (that's half a ton). Wrinkled faces, hairy snouts, and ungainly bodies with paddlelike tails have put them in the category of "so ugly they're cute." Unfortunately, these gentle creatures are an endangered species.

KEEP IN MIND Parking is an additional $3 and the ticket office closes at 4:30, so plan your day accordingly. Also dress in clothing that's okay to get wet. After spending the morning or afternoon here, many visitors head to the beaches of Key Biscayne—routinely voted best in the nation.

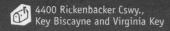 4400 Rickenbacker Cswy.,
Key Biscayne and Virginia Key

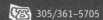 305/361–5705

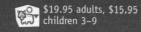 $19.95 adults, $15.95
children 3–9

 Daily 9:30–6

 All ages

or one you feel comfortable leaving outside performance pools. You can also rent strollers on the premises.

Between the six separate shows, check out the other water-themed exhibits, including the manatee exhibit where mothers and their calves of this endangered species frolic. In fact, almost every manatee on the premises is the result of recent rescue and breeding. The Seaquarium frequently provides care for injured manatees, dolphins, and whales.

If your children are over 52 inches in height, then swimming with dolphins might prove an exciting option. It is expensive, however, at $125 per swimmer, plus $32 per observer (children must be observed by a guardian), and reservations should be made at least a week in advance. But this is the kind of experience that can last a lifetime—or at least a childhood. And don't worry if you choose not to swim with your kid. Eight swimmers, four trainers, and anywhere from 3 to 5 dolphins are in the tank at one time, so there's plenty of company, and an emphasis on safety.

KID-FRIENDLY EATS Dining options on Key Biscayne can be rather limited. Check out **Madfish House** (3301 Rickenbacker Cswy., tel. 305/365–9391) for some dockside seafood, or **Bayside Seafood** (3501 Rickenbacker Cswy., tel. 305/361–0808) for tiki hut–style dining complete with conch fritters, fried clams, and peel-and-eat shrimp.

MICCOSUKEE INDIAN VILLAGE

18

I f you've ever wondered how quickly an alligator can move on dry land, then you'll be awed watching some lively 'gator wrestling. Descendants of the Seminoles, the Miccosukee Indians wrestle alligators for show at this authentic Native American village. The trick, apparently, is to grab the alligators by the tail, then flip them onto their backs. Once they're on their backs, they feel helpless and allow the Miccosukees to dominate them. This is dangerous work, and many 'gator wrasslers have the scars to prove it. The wrestling matches are certainly more convincing than the human ones on TV, and children ages 8 and up may want to stay for all the scheduled shows (younger ones may be too frightened).

The Miccosukees moved into the Everglades after leaving a forced resettlement in the 19th century. Deep in the "River of Grass," they learned to live off the land, despite its swampy landscape. In this village, tribal elders live in traditional chickee huts, which have open sides and thatched roofs. Under the shade of these roofs, men and women demonstrate their crafts, such as beading, basket weaving, wood carving, and doll making.

HEY, KIDS! The Tequesta Indians were actually the first to inhabit South Florida, after discovering the area 10,000 years ago, long before Ponce de Leon and other Spanish explorers did in the 1500s. Although the Seminole and Miccosukee Indians didn't arrive in Florida until the 1800s, the locals refer to the Miccosukees as the Indians of South Florida.

 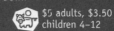

U.S. 41 (Tamiami Trail), 35 mi west of Downtown Miami, Southwest Miami-Dade

$5 adults, $3.50 children 4–12

Daily 9–5

All ages

305/223–8380

Toward the rear of the village, a small museum reflects the Miccosukee's history and culture through artifacts and artwork. Crafts from Miccosukee patchwork and beadwork to Cherokee moccasins and Navajo silver jewelry are on sale at the Miccosukee Gift Shop. A short film explaining the Miccosukee heritage and present position in local politics might appeal to older children interested in American history. The whole family should definitely then cross the street for an airboat ride into the Everglades.

In late July, the Miccosukee Indian Reservation hosts the annual Everglades and Music Festival. A variety of musical entertainment and collections of crafts, arts, and food from surrounding ethnic communities promises a weekend of fun. (Call 305/223–8360 for more information.)

KID-FRIENDLY EATS The **Miccosukee Restaurant** (tel. 305/894–2374) on the premises, adorned inside with beautiful murals depicting Native American life, will win kids over with homemade pumpkin bread, tacos, and standard American cuisine (see Shark Valley).

KEEP IN MIND The Miccosukees also run Miccosukee Indian Gaming (500 S.W. 177th Ave., tel. 305/222–4600), which is a dry-land casino just north of the village. But it's not just for gambling. It has recently been expanded into a five-star hotel and resort with several restaurants and free concerts on the weekends. Besides the music, an arcade will surely keep kids occupied all afternoon, particularly on a rainy day.

MUSEUM OF CONTEMPORARY ART

The MoCA (Museum of Contemporary Art) offers some of the finest pop and modernist art in Miami. Built in 1996, its spiky, art deco design is a marvel in itself, with circular rooms attached to long rectangles of space. Its collection of 20th-century American and European works reaches for the cutting edge. It also hosts traveling exhibits of work by contemporary international artists, and film and video programs feature avant-garde work.

Inside, the museum maintains a busy schedule of eight to 10 annual exhibits. Representative artists range from the contemporary pop pictures of Frank Stella to the brilliant, sparkly clothing designs of Gianni Versace. The museum's philosophy is to present current, living masters alongside eclectic local artists, which makes for a varied experience. Some of the pieces have been donated or loaned by the Rubell family, resident hoteliers whose extensive art collection occupies a museum of its own.

HEY, KIDS!
What someone may think is art you may think is not. Everyone has an opinion, and that opinion counts, especially if it's yours. Don't be afraid to ask tour guides or your folks about paintings that you don't understand, or to compliment those that you really like.

KEEP IN MIND
Some paintings can be almost scary when viewed through a child's eyes. Young kids are more apt to enjoy the exhibits that include collages, film props, and costume designs. Acquaint older children with artists such as Matthew Ritchie, who creates work for the floor and walls, to give them a sense of how anything can be turned into art. Or take them to a show that features more than one artist working in the same medium, which gives them a chance to compare and contrast.

The permanent collection was established in 1994, and continues to grow. The 350 or so pieces currently reflect the artistic climate throughout the United States and abroad, and embrace artistic styles such as Dada and Surrealism. Indeed, exhibits have names such as Sweet Dreams and Nightmares and Inverted Odysseys. Children under the age of 10 may be bewildered by many of the paintings, which can't be taken literally and may need some extensive explanation.

After your museum visit is over, you can explore the antiques stores in North Miami. Most likely, though, your kids would prefer to travel a few miles to the nearby parks, particularly Arch Creek and the Enchanted Forest, to partake in nature and pony-riding activities.

KID-FRIENDLY EATS A short walk away, **Biscayne Wine Merchant & Bistro** (738 N.E. 125th St., tel. 305/899–1997) serves up satisfying plates of pasta among other French-inspired dishes. Take 125th Street east and you'll come across **Tani Guchi's Place** (2224 N.E. 123rd St., tel. 305/892–6744) for fresh kosher sushi.

MUSEUM OF DISCOVERY & SCIENCE

The emphasis is on discovery at this museum in downtown Fort Lauderdale's Arts & Sciences District. Children of almost every age (aside from crawling babies) can feel, touch, and see science for themselves. In fact, the cool hands-on exhibits will have your kids asking, "Are you *sure* this is a museum?"

If you have kids under the age of 7, start your explorations in the Discovery Center. One of the exhibits, the Kids Pick Orange Grove, is solely designed for the little ones—no parents allowed. Here, kids will learn sorting, counting, and hand-eye coordination—but don't tell them that. Just point them in the direction of the fake orange trees, from which they can pick oranges, stack them in crates, and send them for a ride on the mechanical sorter.

Kids will naturally gravitate toward the 52-ft Gravity Clock, made of colorful plastic wheels and pulleys that run on kinetic energy. Then guide them to EcoScapes, where they can wander through a see-through live beehive and examine a captive coral reef, the largest one in the nation. For nondivers, it's the perfect opportunity to examine the give-and-

KEEP IN MIND The museum is a perfect rainy day activity. But if the sun is out, take advantage of the rest of the neighborhood. A historic district, Himmarshee Village fronts the New River, which has paved paths and is a great place to wheel toddlers around. A few blocks to the northeast, a shady expanse with boutiques and outdoor cafés lines Las Olas Boulevard.

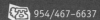

take of ocean life that happens on and around a coral reef system. At Gizmo City, kids can program a robot, lift a 300-pound engine as if it weighed no more than a cup of juice, and smack a virtual volleyball.

The museum also has touch tanks and aquariums—where kids can learn about the natural habitats of sea turtles, alligators, and snakes—and sponsors raise-and-release wildlife programs. Recently, two nurse sharks that had been raised from 12-inch babies—Bruce and the aptly named Baby—were released as full-grown adults into the Atlantic off Fort Lauderdale. But don't think that means your kids won't get a chance to see sharks up-close-and-personal—the museum replaced the two ocean-going nurse sharks with three more babies.

In addition to the 200 permanent exhibits, the museum hosts a variety of traveling exhibits. Call ahead for details.

HEY, KIDS! Baby nurse sharks are called pups. But they don't eat Puppy Chow. At the museum, they're fed the same diet they would eat in the wild: shrimp, crabs, and lobster. This kind of shellfish usually lives on the sea floor, where nurse sharks, called bottom-dwellers, like to hang out.

KID-FRIENDLY EATS The museum café serves sandwiches and drinks. More satisfying eats—and a kid's menu—await at **Big Pink** (300 S.W. First Ave., tel. 954/463– 3755) on the second floor of Las Olas Riverfront, a sibling to the Big Pink diner in Miami. Or head to Las Olas Boulevard and the **Samba Room** (350 E. Las Olas Blvd., tel. 954/468–2000) for Latin-influenced dishes like a *ropa vieja* (shredded meat) sloppy Joe.

NEW WORLD SYMPHONY

Young musicians will be hooked by this orchestra. Since its 1988 debut, the symphony has performed around the world, including New York City's famous Carnegie Hall. Headquartered in South Beach's grand Lincoln Theater, the NWS performs a complete season of entertaining concerts from October to May.

An advanced-training orchestra, the New World provides refuge for musicians ages 21–30 who have graduated from colleges and music seminaries but who have not yet landed professional jobs with resident symphony orchestras. The New World allows them to practice their auditioning skills while at the same time providing a venue for professional-quality performance. When members leave to take jobs in a resident orchestra, other students will fill their places. As you can imagine, entrance into the training orchestra is highly competitive, since it's considered a stepping stone to a symphonic career.

HEY, KIDS!

In an orchestra, each musician contributes a different musical part of a symphony. You may not be impressed with hearing just one part, but when combined with all the other parts, a symphony of sound will unfold before your very ears.

KEEP IN MIND Although family concerts are short and casual, appropriate dress for entrance to Lincoln Theatre is required. Beach attire is not acceptable.

541 Lincoln Rd., South Beach

 305/673-3331

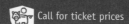 Call for ticket prices

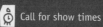 Call for show times

 3 and up

The symphony plays a variety of concerts throughout the season, under the artistic direction of conductor Michael Tilson Thomas. Performances range from chamber group sessions to full-scale symphonic productions. No doubt children who already play instruments will be impressed—the quality of the music put forth is simply astounding and the superb acoustics in the restored art deco Lincoln Theatre resonate throughout the concert hall.

For kids who have never played an instrument or even seen a classical concert, the New World is an excellent introduction. Throughout the season, the orchestra presents family concerts, accompanied by programs that describe everything from the individual instruments to concert etiquette (no candy-wrapper crumpling!). On holidays and some Sundays, the orchestra broadcasts the concert outside to the whole of Lincoln Road, and even the pigeons stop their perpetual pecking to listen up.

KID-FRIENDLY EATS You can eat at any of the numerous sidewalk cafés lining Lincoln Road. A favorite spot after a concert, **Café Papillon** (530 Lincoln Rd., tel. 305/673–1139) serves terrific focaccia sandwiches and homemade soup daily.

OLETA RIVER STATE RECREATION AREA

A local favorite, this 1,000-acre park is smack-dab in the middle of urbanity. But once you're in the park, you don't see or hear anything that says 21st century (unless you count the cars in the parking lot). You wouldn't even know that the natural lagoon-style, low-impact beach was constructed, but your preschoolers and toddlers will appreciate the lack of surf that enables them to play in the shallows without being knocked over.

The park is on both the Oleta River, hence its name, and the Intracoastal Waterway, so the H2O is brackish if not downright salty. Both the water and the relative quiet attract the rarely visible West Indian manatee. Schools of porpoises also find it a welcome place to frolic, and delightfully impress children with their leaps and jumps. For a closer look, rent kayaks, which ride so low in the water kids will almost feel like they're swimming with dolphins.

KID-FRIENDLY EATS Across the street from the park, a variety of ethnic restaurants can be found in the strip malls. For sushi, **Hiro Japanese Restaurant** (3007 N.E. 163rd St., tel. 305/948–3687) is always a fresh bet and the yakitori menu delights young nibblers. To the east, kids have a blast (and perhaps a stomachache afterward) at **Emerald Coast** (16850 Collins Ave., Sunny Isles Beach, tel. 305/787–1530), an eat-your-fill Chinese buffet restaurant with hundreds of items. Go for the novelty if nothing else.

3400 N.E. 163rd St., North Miami Beach

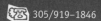 305/919-1846

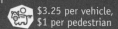 $3.25 per vehicle,
$1 per pedestrian

 Daily 8–sunset

 All ages

Wildlife viewing isn't limited to the water. Furrier mammals are attracted to the forests that surround the waterways, and children will almost always be surprised when an unexpected visitor—raccoon, possum, fox, or squirrel—crosses their path.

Last, but certainly not least, the park is a great place for other forms of entertainment. If your kids want to bike, Oleta has some of the most challenging trails in Miami. Remind your kids to watch for the mangrove roots, which pop out of the ground or grow in shallow water. Budding anglers can also cast off a 90-ft pier and catch snapper, grouper, or grunt. Pavilions with picnic tables are scattered throughout the park, and 14 unadorned log cabins provide adequate facilities. The park's truly the place for roughing it, but it's not much for spontaneity. If you want to camp, call ahead for reservations.

HEY, KIDS! Manatees in some ways resemble porpoises. They're both sleek, long, and have flippers. But you'll know what you're seeing soon enough—porpoises jump and manatees float lazily in the water. Keep your eyes peeled!

KEEP IN MIND Be sure to ask for a map when you stop to pay at the park gate. This will help you choose activities for the day. Don't feel you have to do everything. The park is too large to cover in a single afternoon, plus you can always return another day.

PARROT JUNGLE AND GARDENS

Can you say "Polly wants a cracker?" Good—so can an excellent percentage of the approximately 2,000 exotic birds housed in this aviary and botanical gardens. But the parrots, cockatoos, and macaws here do more than talk. In a mini-amphitheater, they also ride bicycles and roller-skate, tricks usually associated with circus dogs. But then, this place can easily seem like a circus, especially in the cooler hours of the morning and late afternoon, when the birds are not only active but vocal.

Despite the name, this 12-acre space isn't all about birds. Stroll the paved, stroller-friendly winding paths and you'll come across more than 1,000 species of plants, including a collection of exotic orchids. When the bald cypress and oak trees meet overhead, and ferns and flowering plants spill onto the paths, your kids really will feel like they're lost in the jungle—that is, until they hit the cactus garden. The many twists and turns provide occasional pockets of privacy even when the attraction is crowded. Stop for a moment and see if your older children can identify the bird calls.

KEEP IN MIND The lush jungles are a full morning or afternoon activity; most folks spend an average of three hours here. Make sure to call the complex first before visiting. As of this writing, Parrot Jungle has purchased new land so not all animals may be housed on the premises during the time of your visit.

KID-FRIENDLY EATS A restaurant on the premises, the **Parrot Café** (tel. 305/666–7834) can satisfy immediate breakfast, lunch, and snack needs with an assortment of fast-food items. If you're looking for something slightly more sit-down, head to **Picnics at Allen's Drugstore** (4000 Red Rd., tel. 305/665–6964), an old-fashioned drugstore-diner where kids can watch their BLTs and chili dogs being made.

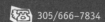 11000 S.W. 57th Ave., Coral Gables

 $12.95 adults,
$8.95 children 3–10

Daily 9:30–6

305/666-7834

All ages

In other exhibits, somnolent alligators soak and flamingos wade off in the distance. A children's petting zoo contains baby goats, pigs, and other tame farm animals whose baby fuzz invites little hands. Be careful, though. Some of these fellows are more than half grown, and could bowl over an unsuspecting toddler.

Snakes, such as boa constrictors, are also abundant, and the staff frequently takes them out of their cages and shows them to the crowds. Kids who have worked up the courage are usually permitted to stroke them, too. Shows such as the Creatures in the Mist present even more reptiles, mostly tortoises, iguanas, and such mammals as squirrel monkeys or three-toed sloths, whose home is the Amazon rain forest. Too bad the animals you want to touch most are off-limits to visitors, but if you're lucky, you'll be right on time to see the baby gibbons frolic with the staff. They can practically jump rope over their own arms.

HEY, KIDS! Buy some sunflower seeds, place them in the palm of your hand, and voila! You're a parrot's best friend. Their beaks look a little fierce, but you'll be amazed how gentle these colorful birds can be as long as you hold your hand still. The only birds who probably won't eat these treats are the flamingos. They feast on shrimp, which is where they get their pink color.

REDLAND FRUIT AND SPICE PARK

A one-of-a-kind park, this 30-acre complex allows children to see where oranges, mangoes, and bananas come from. Inaugurated in 1944, this park has more than 500 varieties of vegetables, fruits, nuts, spices, and herbs from around the world, including 65 types of bananas and 40 kinds of grapes. How do you choose which one to eat?

Well, technically you can't. The rules of the park are this: You can nosh on any fruit that has already fallen to the ground, but you can't pick any. So you have to rely on nature's handouts. You also can't take any fruit out of the park, so arrive with an empty stomach to sample your favorite fruit, providing it's in season. Plants and trees are arranged by country of origin. You can also take an informative tour, which includes samplings, sniffings, and handlings of exotic fruits and nuts, or purchase a copy of *A Pioneer History of the Fruit and Spice Park* at the store, which gives background info on this park.

KID-FRIENDLY EATS A little fruit can go a long way, but probably not long enough to last your kids back to Miami. If that's the case, hit the **Pollo Tropical** (915 Homestead Blvd., tel. 305/245–0410) for citrus-marinated grilled chicken before you head home, or stop on the way back at the **Old Cutler Oyster Co.** (18415 S. Dixie Hwy., Cutler Ridge, tel. 305/238–2051) for fried oysters and clams.

 14801 S.W. 187th Ave., Homestead

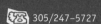 305/247–5727

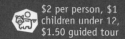 $2 per person, $1 children under 12, $1.50 guided tour

 Daily 10–5

 All ages

Kids love wandering around here, and they tend to pick up a little horticulture along with the avocados. But the park is also perfect for very young children, since an 8-ft-wide paved path is stroller- and wheelchair-accessible and rest rooms are handy and clean. Although fruit trees provide plenty of shade, the sun can spot you through the leaves, so remember to lather up yourself and the little ones with sunscreen.

Finally, you can take a bit of the park home with you. If you visit the Redland Fruit Store on your way out, you can buy canned fruits, jams, jellies, preserves, spices, cookbooks, and reference books. You and your children can also put your newfound gardening knowledge to use by purchasing seeds and/or cuttings to plant in your own backyard.

HEY, KIDS! Feel free to touch and explore in this park. Just remember the rules, and pay attention to the signs. If an area is off-limits, respect the signs and head elsewhere to play.

KEEP IN MIND The park has some poisonous plants, which are carefully marked and guarded. Remind your children not to put anything in their mouths except the fruit or vegetable they want to eat. Also keep an eye on toddlers who might inadvertently swallow and choke on small nuts and seeds.

ROBERT IS HERE

Ever hear of a carambola? An egg fruit? A monstera deliciosa? Well if you haven't, chances are Robert Is Here has. True enough, a visit to a roadside fruit stand may not seem like the ideal family excursion at first, but kids will warm to Robert's quirky and friendly personality. He's become somewhat of a minor celebrity, appearing on national news and talk shows, hawking his tropical fruits. The curious kids may even want to take a peek in the back of the stand at one of the largest collections of tortoises in the world.

This family-owned fruit stand began when Robert's father, a farmer, had a surplus of cucumbers he couldn't sell on the market. So he put 7-year-old Robert on the side of the road with a sign saying "Robert Is Here," and the fruit stand was born. Almost 40 years later, the stand has broadened its original selection by offering dozens of varieties of exotic tropical fruits and vegetables. If you don't recognize something while you're browsing among the fragrant specimens, some of which look like they might've come from the moon, ask.

HEY, KIDS!

A carambola is also called a star fruit. If you cut this spiky yellow fruit, starting at the narrow end, the slices will look like five-pointed stars. The flavor of the carambola is very tart—perfect if you like sour candy and gum.

KEEP IN MIND

Homestead is farm country. For a break from the miles of sometimes monotonous countryside, stop at a U-pick farm, hand the kids a basket, and tell 'em to get to work. Depending on the season, even the youngest kids can pick strawberries, key limes, cucumbers, tomatoes, and other local fruits and vegetables.

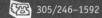

The staff is happy to explain and even give you a taste of whatever it is you're pointing at. On one side of the stand, kids can wander among homemade treats, including Robert's mom's mango preserves and his own key lime pie. The staff specializes in whipping up frothy key lime milk shakes and offering recipes for both the smoothie and another house specialty, mango cake.

Along with fruits and veggies comes a host of free advice. Want to find out the best place to catch an airboat ride? Robert Is Here knows. Want to find a good restaurant for a kid-friendly lunch? Robert Is Here can tell you. Just don't forget to grab a *monstera deliciosa* before you hit the road (in the direction Robert tells you to go, of course). This enormous fruit, which looks like a long, green, scaly alligator tail, is actually a product of the philodendron plant and has a pleasant flavor much like a cross between a pineapple and a banana.

KID-FRIENDLY EATS Nothing works up an appetite like picking fruit. Satisfy those hungry tummies at **Shiver's Bar-B-Q** (28001 So. Dixie Hwy., tel. 305/248–2272) with some fall-off-the-bone beef ribs, just the ticket when you're tired to the bone.

SANFORD L. ZIFF JEWISH
MUSEUM OF FLORIDA

Instead of focusing on the more graphic and disturbing aspects of Jewish history, this museum is designed as a quick history lesson for children of all religions. Housed in a former synagogue with 80 stained-glass windows, a copper dome, a marble stage, and art deco archways, the exhibits focus on Jewish culture. The permanent exhibit, Mosaic: Jewish Life in Florida, showcases more than 500 photos of Eastern European Jews and artifacts, such as pieces of clothing, books, and jewelry, which examines Jewish life in Florida for the past 2½ centuries.

None of the exhibits is really graphic, but some are sad. Barely a Minyan: The Last Jewish Elderly of South Beach displays a collection of Old World photos, while Jews, Germany, Memory: A Contemporary Portrait addresses fallout from the Holocaust and Jewish life in Germany today. Most of the photos are in black-and-white or sepia tones. You can pick up museum brochures and books at the front desk to determine which sites are appropriate for your kids, but be aware that some of this material costs extra.

KEEP IN MIND This museum is on the smallish side, and while there's plenty of history to examine, a tour (guided tours are available on request) probably won't take more than an hour. On the plus side, the section of South Beach where the museum is has plenty of street parking (bring lots of change) and it's just a two-block walk to the beach. That makes getting cultured *and* tan in the same day a distinct possibility.

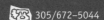 301 Washington Ave., South Beach

 $5 adults, $2.50 children 6–17, $10 family

T–Su 10–5, closed M and Jewish holidays

 305/672–5044

8 and up

Not all the exhibits take a serious look at things or even a firmly Jewish perspective. Yeast of Eden: Ethnic Breads in Florida is a charming take on the state's present ethnic diversity. A life-size house built with shellacked breads and bread products—bagels, baguettes, even Cheerios—gives new meaning to community building. The house is also plastered with drawings, recipes, and photographs donated by the same schoolchildren who labored over this fascinating little cottage. In fact, all that's missing is the scent of fresh-baked bread—but then, perhaps that would have been too tempting for the noshers.

HEY, KIDS! See if you can piece together stories from the exhibits, such as how Jews got to America, whether or not they were accepted, and how they tried to fit in.

KID-FRIENDLY EATS One block east and one block south lies a trendy diner called **Big Pink** (157 Collins Ave., tel. 305/531–0888), run by renowned chef-proprietor Michael Schwartz (of the upscale Nemo across the street). The something-for-everybody menu caters to kids with a special menu, crayons, and indestructible Lucite tables, and to big people with noteworthy gourmet flair.

SHARK VALLEY

Contrary to its unusual name, Shark Valley is home to those long, toothy reptiles that populate the Everglades—the American alligator. You'll know you're in the right place when you start passing 'gators tanning themselves on the side of the highway.

Once in the park, you might see an alligator or two on the pathways instead of in the canals. Since humans aren't their typical prey, they'll ignore you if you ignore them. And most alligators will go out of their way to avoid you. But if you find one on the path that you simply can't get around, exercise caution and inform the guides at the Visitor Center before proceeding.

A paved path called the Tram Road cuts through the saw grass plains and allows you to hike, tram, or bike 15 looping mi through the Everglades. On either side of the path, water comes right up to the edge, and alligators are so prevalent that children who start to keep track of each 'gator they spot often lose count by the end of the day. Kids with cameras can take close-up pictures of the hatchlings, usually found in the

KID-FRIENDLY EATS Just across the street is the **Miccosukee Restaurant** (Tamiami Trail, tel. 305/223–8380), where you can sample authentic fry bread (dough deep-fried in peanut oil), deep-fried frogs' legs, a delicacy around these parts, and hamburgers.

KEEP IN MIND You're on your own if you hike or bike through the park. Although Shark Valley is considered extremely safe, don't allow children to wander alone anywhere in this park, especially near water in South Florida (the tiniest drainage canal could host an alligator or two). Although alligators don't approach humans, you should always keep a minimum of 15 ft away from them at all times. For the most part, the alligators ignore you, but they can be nasty when provoked. And if anything falls in the water, do not retrieve it. Don't forget insect repellent, preferably with sunscreen in it.

shallow waters by the drainage canals where they hide from bigger 'gators, as well as specimens of up to about 8 ft, drifting in the water or sunning on the banks.

Whether you ride or walk, check in at the visitor center first to get a listing of the wildlife you can see. Guided tram tours last about two hours and include frequent stops for wildlife photo opportunities. You can also rent bicycles from the Shark Valley Tram Tour company at the visitor center. Make sure you stop at the observation tower at the midway point for an 18-mi panoramic view of the park. Alligators as long as 20 ft have been spotted.

For a shorter sampler of the park, check out the two smaller self-guided trails behind the visitor center. Bobcat Boardwalk is a half-mile tour through saw grass slough and tropical hardwood forests, and the Otter Cave Hammock Trail, a quarter-mile limestone trail, winds through a lush, tropical hardwood forest. Both are wheelchair accessible, but like the Tram Road, can be prone to flooding during the summer rainy season (April through November). Always call ahead for conditions.

HEY, KIDS! Although it's rare to see them, white-tail deer and the endangered Florida panther make their homes in the Everglades. When you take a tram ride, keep your eyes focused on the clumps of trees called hammocks that break up the swamp. If you're lucky, you just might make out a deer or two, camouflaged against the hardwood. If you're really lucky, you might even spot a panther off in the distance (see above for tram rides). Since this is a 15 mile trail that goes deep into the Everglades, binoculars are helpful.

SHOPS AT SUNSET PLACE

A mall is a mall is a mall, say the parents. Teens, of course, think differently, and in Miami, mall culture abounds. In other words, kids like to hang out here, mostly for each other's company, but occasionally for the shopping and restaurants. The mall's expansive tri-level courtyards and lush, tropical landscaping provide plenty of activities for sunny and rainy days.

Kids will quickly notice that everything is bigger and better here. This 502,000-square-ft mall is the largest and most modern outdoor shopping center in Miami. The structure is something of a wonder—a convoluted art deco castle, it glows with a variety of pastel colors. The interior is a bit difficult to navigate, with many dead ends and loops, which can make good hide-and-seek fun.

Teens won't have a problem navigating this mall, however, especially when they see the illuminated signs of shops galore, including such chains as Virgin Records Megastore and

HEY, KIDS! The art deco style of architecture is notable for round windows, similar to the ones found on ships, decorative swoops and bannister-like curls, and arched doorways. Art deco buildings are almost always painted in several pastel colors. It's not unusual to see one building that has pink or yellow walls and trim painted in anything from purple to orange.

 5701 Sunset Dr., South Miami

 Free

 Daily 10–10

317/636–1600

 All ages

NikeTown. Nonshoppers will immediately gravitate to Gameworks, where a plethora of arcade and virtual reality games will keep them occupied for potentially hours on end.

No visit to this mall would be complete, however, without being enveloped by a thrilling IMAX theater show that depicts the natural wonders of the Earth and sea. It puts nature into a stunning perspective that will surely entertain.

The University of Miami is right across the highway, so the mall can be a good diversion for children not yet in middle school while high-schoolers visit the college and tour the campus. The museum or historic homes in nearby Coconut Grove and Downtown Miami are good starters—a bit of history first, then a lot of fun!

KID-FRIENDLY EATS

On the bottom floor of the mall, the **Wilderness Café** (tel. 305/669–4426) mimics a Rainforest Café theme, but the food is decidedly Australian influenced, with lots of beef on the menu. A few doors away, **Sweet Donna's Country Store** (tel. 305/740–9322) has the best macaroni-and-cheese in the city, homemade bread, and gargantuan desserts.

TRANSPORTATION

The mall is easy to find, poised as it is on the southeast corner of U.S. 1 and Red Road. It also has plenty of reasonably priced parking in a covered, adjacent lot. Just turn left on Red Road and then make a right into the mall complex. Follow signs past the movie theaters to the parking lot.

SOUTH BEACH ART DECO DISTRICT

O fficially known as the Art Deco District, the three parallel avenues that comprise this part of South Beach are exciting for children of all ages. The action in this part of town, which borders the white-sand beaches, is constant. The area comprises 1 square mi of many brightly colored buildings, painted in memorable, decorative pastels.

Ocean Drive, which lines the Atlantic Ocean, is the most distinct avenue and showcases some of the best examples of art deco around—porthole windows, spiral staircases, shipboard flourishes. It's also best for kids 4 and under, who may get bored with strolling and want to take a swim break or build a sand castle. The beach, after all, is only steps away. Later in the afternoon, you can head back to the hotels and cafés on Ocean Drive, most of which have been carefully restored and listed as National Historic Landmarks. Almost all of them are open to the sidewalk. A Mardi Gras atmosphere pervades every day and night of the week here. You wouldn't want to book a room, but you would want to spend a day or two alternating between Ocean Drive beaches (think white sand and azure water) and cafés.

KEEP IN MIND South Beach and the Art Deco District define the word "party." Both boys and girls wear very little, and lifestyles are extremely open. Enjoy the show, but try not to get too involved. Plus, if your kids are little, you might want to spend more time on Lincoln Road, which is more family-friendy.

KID-FRIENDLY EATS Ocean Drive offers numerous outdoor dining options, though most of them are mediocre. For ethnic interest with a little celebrity flair, check out Gloria Estefan's Cuban restaurant **Lario's on the Beach** (820 Ocean Dr., tel. 305/532–9577) or Ricky Martin's Puerto Rican eatery **Casa Salsa** (524 Ocean Dr., tel. 305/604–5959). On Collins Avenue, **Sushi Rock Café** (1351 Collins Ave., tel. 305/532–2133) serves up outstanding sushi.

From 6th to 23rd Sts. and Lennox Ave. to Ocean Dr., South Beach

Free

n/a

n/a

All ages

One block over, Collins Avenue has its own personality, riveting for preteens and teens. Many clothing designers have set up shop here, selling stylish, trendy, and form-fitting wear for outlandish prices. The hotels lining this avenue are both quieter than the ones on Ocean Drive and more elaborate. Restructured gems such as the Delano and the National are havens for celebrities, and both have popular cafés that hum with activity.

Another block to the west, Washington Avenue is the late-night hot spot. Restaurants, nightclubs, and eclectic boutiques rage from late evening to the early morning hours. Some of the beach's best eateries are here, and are more sedate than the frantic cafés on Ocean Drive. Locals tend to frequent this part of the Art Deco District more often as well, especially in the early parts of the evening when the hype hasn't hit yet. During the day, these places can be fine for children, but evening is reserved for the club-going set.

HEY, KIDS! South Beach is named for its beaches, and these wide, sandy expanses are some of the best in town. Build a sand castle, fly a kite, or go swimming in water as warm as your bath. Be careful not to swim when lifeguards aren't on duty, though, especially when signs are posted that say "riptides." Riptides are currents that can catch you up and take you out to sea. If you do get caught in one, don't panic, and under no circumstances try to swim back to the beach. Instead, swim parallel to the beach.

SOUTHERN GLADES TRAIL

6

Although cycling in Miami might seem like a hazardous proposition, given traffic congestion and the lack of bike trails, this path provides a safe sojourn for the family who bikes. This trail was created accidentally, when the U.S. Army Corps of Engineers tore down the wall of the C-111 canal to help restore the natural flow of the Everglades. It also restored space, which the Redland Conservancy used to create this new installment of the South Dade Greenway Network, which connects to three other bike paths.

You'll have to drive to the starting point of this 14-mi vista. Then saddle up and take the path toward the Everglades National Park entrance. The predominantly flat trail leads past farmland and saw grass expanses, following the twists and turns of one of the largest canals in South Florida. Make sure the kids have helmets on, because the path is unpaved and can be quite hard during the dry season (November–March). During the rainy season,

HEY, KIDS! Turkey vultures got their name because they look like turkeys, though some argue they resemble roosters more. Locals used these eye-catching birds to mark the seasons. You know it's officially winter when the turkey vultures, who migrate long distances to South Florida every year, come to roost. About April, they'll start heading back to the west coast, where spring is in full flower.

the path may occasionally be obscured, so exercise common sense when heading down here. Remind kids to be courteous and stay to the right. The path also attracts horses and their riders, as well as a few hikers.

During your ride, be sure to make plenty of stops to view wildlife. Although you probably won't see quite as many 'gators as you would in the Everglades, you may spot fish, turtles, and snakes in the canals along the trail. In the quiet early mornings and late afternoons, the wading birds such as the great blue heron flock to the water. At other times of the day, you will still have plenty of bird-watching. Roseate spoonbills, ospreys, and turkey vultures, which are common here but unusual elsewhere, flutter about along the trail.

KID-FRIENDLY EATS Eats are scarce around here, so your best bet is to pack plenty of drinks and snacks. After the ride, stop at **Viet Family Restaurant** (15892 S.W. 137th Ave., Southwest Miami-Dade, tel. 305/259–8508) for home-style Vietnamese noodle soups and spring rolls.

KEEP IN MIND The best time to ride is early in the morning or late in the afternoon, when the wading birds start looking for something yummy to eat. By avoiding the middle of the day, you'll also escape the noon sun, which can be brutal even during the cooler winter months.

TEMPLE BETH AM CONCERT SERIES

More than a concert series, this is a social outing appropriate for the whole family to enjoy. Although held in a modern temple, the music—opera, jazz, and classical—performed here is not only secular but is designed as a great introduction for younger children, who may be starting to appreciate all types of music and even play an instrument themselves. If they don't already play, the music here may encourage them to learn.

Who's performing depends on the series that year. In the past, kids have been able to hear the Florida Philharmonic Orchestra and the New World Symphony. To keep younger children thoroughly entertained, musicians stop to explain their instruments, tell jokes, or regale related stories. In addition, concerts are usually specialized to introduce genres of music such as with the percussion show or the introduction to jazz concert.

KID-FRIENDLY EATS This section of town has many pit stops for refueling. You can drive to **Fuji Hana** (11768 N. Kendall Dr., tel. 305/275–9003) for sushi, or head back to **Grazie Café** (11523 S. Dixie Hwy., Pinecrest, tel. 305/232–5533) for a plate of homemade ravioli followed by tiramisu.

HEY, KIDS! When you hear someone refer to a brass instrument, they're usually talking about those brightly colored, gold-hued instruments such as trumpets, trombones, and tubas. If someone mentions woodwind instruments, they're referring to instruments such as flutes or clarinets, which used to be made of wood. Today, however, they're made of plastic or metal. With the exception of the flute, the woodwind family has reeds for mouthpieces. Finally, don't let the saxophone fool you. It's colored like a brass instrument, but technically it's a woodwind because it has a reed.

 5950 N. Kendall Dr., Kendall

 305/667-6667

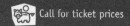 Call for ticket prices

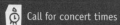 Call for concert times

 5 and up

The concert series is a sincere educational opportunity. Parents can instruct their children in the art of listening without fidgeting and prepare them for attending more sophisticated shows and concerts in other venues. The good news is that if little ones do fuss, no one else in the audience minds, since mostly everyone there has the same motive—to expose young children to music other than Barney tunes and lullabies. In addition, audiences tend to just want to have a good time, so you'll hear plenty of hand-clapping on the more jazzy and percussion numbers. You may even see your youngest get up and dance.

Concerts rarely last longer than an hour, and cookies and juice are provided afterward. Parents also like to congregate with like-minded guardians, so plan on spending at least two hours here.

TRANSPORTATION Because public transportation is practically nonexistent, you'll have to drive to the temple. If you're heading north on U.S. 1, make a left on North Kendall Drive; if you're heading south, make a right. Just be aware that North Kendall Drive also goes by its number name, 88th Street.

VENETIAN POOL

4

Although this pool's elegantly designed caves, waterfalls, and stone bridges may seem out of sync with the miles of sandy beaches that define Miami, it is no less enjoyable for water frolics. In fact, the pool and its castlelike surroundings attract local and national photographers, who love to use its appealing setting for photo shoots.

This 820,000-gallon pool, fed daily by fresh spring water, began life as an unsightly coral rock quarry in 1923. When Denman Fink, uncle of founding father of Coral Gables, George Merrick, was commissioned to build the pool, he enlisted Phineas Paist, who added Venetian-style flourishes to the buildings that bank the site. Today, the pool provides stellar underwater fun for good swimmers over the age of 5. Kids can wiggle through the grottoes and explore the underwater caves (if they're good at holding their breath, that is), and it's ideal for playing water games such as Marco Polo because of its twists and turns.

HEY, KIDS! Coral Gables is frequently called the City Beautiful. Founder and realtor George Merrick named the streets for Spanish cities and explorers, and hired architects to build his vision of a Spanish city. Many of those architects used the stones quarried from the Venetian Pool for the local houses. Merrick never quite saw his vision fulfilled, due to a disastrous hurricane followed by the Great Depression, but city leaders have since passed design laws to make sure Merrick's dreams have come—and stayed—true.

Once kids are out of the water, it might be a little difficult to keep track of them. Older kids might disappear for impromptu showers under one of the two waterfalls, while younger ones might be found building a sand castle on the man-made beach or playing pirates on the "desert island," a palm-tree-fringed island attached to the "mainland" by a cobblestone bridge. The teenagers might be relaxing in the shade of the porticos and loggias for a little people-watching. One thing's for sure: Once your family is installed at the Venetian Pool, it'd take Marco Polo himself—or sundown, perhaps—to dislodge them.

For older children and adults, the Venetian Aquatic Club, a volunteer group, teaches all levels of swimming lessons. Water aerobics, snorkeling, and scuba diving classes are a terrific option if you're planning on exploring any of the artificial reef sites around Miami.

KID-FRIENDLY EATS The pool has its own little gourmet café called, appropriately enough, **The Café at Venetian Pool** (tel. 305/460-5356). Kid-inspired eats include mozzarella sticks, chicken fingers, Philly cheese-steak hoagies, and lasagna-of-the-week.

KEEP IN MIND Swimming through caves can be confusing for young swimmers. Remind your children if they get confused about direction, look for sunlight and swim toward it. The Venetian Pool is fed daily by clean, cool spring water, so children under 3 are not allowed in the complex at all.

VIZCAYA MUSEUM AND GARDENS

3

Kids will marvel at this Italian Renaissance-style villa. Not only will its history pique their interest but its 34 rooms stocked with furniture, textiles, sculptures, and paintings from the 15th century are bound to astound. They'll also be amazed to learn that the owner, James Deering, only lived here in the winter.

Son of the founder of Deering Harvesting Machine Company and International Harvester, and brother of Charles (*see* the Charles Deering Estate), Deering built this home in 1916 just to show off his wealth and impress the locals. It worked. Nearly 100 years later, the house has been preserved as a museum, and the lush, tropical gardens fronting Biscayne Bay have been lovingly tended. Residents enjoy holding events here, and weddings and other private parties frequently light up the place in the evenings. Because most events are held after-hours, though, visitors don't have to worry about being shut out of the villa.

HEY, KIDS!

Vizcaya is often used as a movie set. In fact, a portion of the memorable comedy *Ace Ventua: Pet Detective*, involving a hapless pet detective played by Jim Carrey, was shot here. See if you can find a certain famous bathroom.

KEEP IN MIND The Miami Museum of Science & Space Transit Planterarium is practically next door, so dual activities separated by lunch might be called for if you have the stamina. You can also drive around the neighborhood toward Coconut Grove. Sly Stallone's former mansion is located in this part of town; other grand houses, some completely made of coral, belong to the wealthy un-famous residents.

Guided tours last 45 minutes, or you can grab a handbook and explore on your own. Either way, you should observe the rug where Christopher Columbus once stood, and check out the telephone booth (kids under 12 who have never seen anything but touch-tone might be surprised). A few architectural oddities include doors that close as slowly as a manatee swims through a canal; Deering didn't like doors slamming in the wind, so he designed them to creak shut quietly. Of course, the continuous breeze off the bay is no longer an issue—high-rise condominiums built in Coconut Grove tend to block the wind as effectively as mountains protect a valley.

KID-FRIENDLY EATS You can drive into the center of Coconut Grove, where plenty of chain-restaurant options such as **Johnny Rockets** (3036 Grand Ave., Coconut Grove, tel. 305/444–1000) and the **Cheesecake Factory** (3015 Grand Ave., Coconut Grove, tel. 305/447–9898) abound. If you're looking for something with a little more character, head the other way toward downtown and the **Firehouse Four** (1000 S. Miami Ave., Miami, tel. 305/371–3473), an expansive restaurant inside in a restored 1930's firehouse.

WEEKS AIR MUSEUM

Many children dream of flying, and this museum—begun by aviator, champion aerobatic, and aircraft designer Kermit Weeks in 1985—caters to their fantasy of flight, providing history of how we came to conquer gravity and fly.

At the Tamiami Airport, this museum is dedicated to preserving antique airplanes. A comprehensive history written on placards accompanies each plane. For example, the North American P-51 Mustang was a trim fighter plane designed and built toward the end of WW II. The museum houses the P-51D, the fourth version of the plane, of which 7,956 were built. The popular Grumman Duck, an amphibian used for search-and-rescue missions, is one of only 600 made, while Lockheed P-38 Lightning contains descriptions of actual battles it fought. Young history buffs, who may have studied the subject already, will find these tales of flight thrilling.

HEY, KIDS! An antique aircraft can cost up to $1 million and 50,000 hours in labor to restore. You can get an idea of how intricate the work is by putting together a model airplane yourself. Keep a log and don't ask for help from your parents or friends. When you're finished, add up all your hours. They may not come close to 50,000, but it's still probably a good amount.

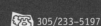 14710 S.W. 128th St., Kendall

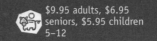 $9.95 adults, $6.95 seniors, $5.95 children 5–12

 Daily 10–5

 All ages

305/233–5197

Younger kids, especially those under the age of 7, may have little interest in analyzing these archaic machines, but they'll still enjoy gazing at them. If you have extra funds, you can certainly spice up the day by booking a "mission" on a T-6 military trainer or a classic Howard DGA-15. The flights are open to passengers of all ages, though the noise of the propellers may startle young children. Call Air Sal at the Tamiami Airport (tel. 305/251–1982) for more information.

Several events are held at the museum throughout the year, and though some may involve wings, they don't all involve planes. For example, the Corvette & Wings Show showcases vintage Corvettes from all over the state, and the Sunrise Balloon Race takes place annually in May. If you're planning a visit to the antique aircraft, call first to make sure the museum is operating on normal hours.

KID-FRIENDLY EATS The museum concession serves coffee, baked goods, and snacks. But for something more substantial, try **The Fish House** (10000 S.W. 56th St., tel. 305/595–8453) for the fresh catch of the day. It's a bit of a drive but worth it.

KEEP IN MIND Tamiami Airport is a busy, working airport. You'll want to avoid driving here during rush hour—the traffic in this part of town is quite heavy—and during popular flight arrivals and departure, such as on Friday or Sunday afternoon and evening.

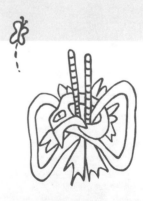

WRECK TREK

A nywhere you look in Miami, you see water: Biscayne Bay, the Intracoastal Waterway, lakes, canals, and pools. But to see *under* the aquamarine-hued H2O requires just a little more involvement. In other words, for certified divers 10 and up to really view what's going on down there, they have to don masks, fins, and tanks—and dive.

The plan of the Artificial Reef Program was that man-made objects would be stripped of dangerous parts, securely bolted to the ocean floor, and gradually become a safe host for both marine life and visiting humans, especially families. Over the years, the program's directors have sunk a variety of man-made objects, including boats, military tanks, oil rigs, and even an airplane—that's right, a Boeing 727 jet called the *Spirit of Miami*. Lowered to a depth of 82 ft in front of a national, televised audience, the *Spirit* is an excellent artificial reef site for novice and experienced divers.

HEY, KIDS!

The hordes of colorful, tropical fish down here can make busy Miami look like a ghost town in comparison. But remember to keep your hands—and fins—to yourself when it comes to marine life. Most fish are a little fussy about being touched. And never, ever dive without a partner, who can help you if you get into trouble.

KEEP IN MIND

Water temperatures vary from 70°F to 80°F. While that sounds warm, kids can get chilled in these waters quickly if they're not wearing wet suits, especially during the winter. Also make sure to sign up for guided dives, with boats that are operated in accordance with U.S. Coast Guard regulations and licensed captains. For more information about dive packages, check with local dive shops or call 888/SCUBA–MB. The Miami Beach Marina, Crandon Marina, and Haulover Marina will all have information about tour departures and destinations; remember prices will vary according to boat, captain, and destination.

Still, most local aficionados agree that the fondly nicknamed Wreck Trek is not only one of the most intriguing dives around, but one of the most easily handled. (Kids can learn to snorkel and dive by the age of 6 in Florida but unless their skills are superior, this one's best handled by older children.)

Just off North Miami Beach, the Wreck Trek is a triad of three artificial wrecks—the 85-ft tugboat *Patricia*, the 100-ft fishing boat *Miss Karline*, and the Radio Antenna, an old Radio Mambi antenna. In addition, the underwater trails connecting the main wrecks (several smaller boats are down here, too) make it hard for the youngest of the pack to get lost. And if you do, you can always make arrangements to meet your family back at the Antenna—its numerous welded peaks make it difficult to miss.

KID-FRIENDLY EATS Diving's hungry work, but chances are kids aren't going to want fish when they come up for air. So if you're diving the Wreck Trek, once back on land take them for delicatessen fare at the landmark **Wolfie Cohen's Rascal House** (17190 Collins Ave., tel. 305/947–4581) or for Mexican food at the colorful **Paquito's** (16265 Biscayne Blvd., tel. 305/947–5027).

games

THE CLASSICS

"I'M THINKING OF AN ANIMAL..." With older kids you can play 20 Questions: Have your leader think of an animal, vegetable, or mineral (or, alternatively, a person, place, or thing) and let everybody else try to guess what it is. The correct guesser takes over as leader. If no one figures out the secret within 20 questions, the first person goes again. With younger children, limit the guessing to animals and don't put a ceiling on how many questions can be asked. With rivalrous siblings, just take turns being leader. Make the game's theme things you expect to see at your day's destination.

"I SEE SOMETHING YOU DON'T SEE AND IT IS BLUE."
Stuck for a way to get your youngsters to settle down in a museum? Sit them down on a bench in the middle of a room and play this vintage favorite. The leader gives just one clue—the color—and everybody guesses away.

FUN WITH THE ALPHABET

"I'M GOING TO THE GROCERY..." The first player begins, "I'm going to the grocery and I'm going to buy... " and finishes the sentence with the name of an object, found in grocery stores, that begins with the letter "A". The second player repeats what the first player has said, and adds the name of another item that starts with "B". The third player repeats everything that has been said so far and adds something that begins with "C" and so on through the alphabet. Anyone who skips or misremembers an item is out (or decide up front that you'll give hints to all who need 'em). You can modify the theme depending on where you're going that day, as "I'm going to X and I'm going to see..."

"I'M GOING TO ASIA ON AN ANT TO ACT UP." Working their way through the alphabet, players concoct silly sentences stating where they're going, how they're traveling, and what they'll do.

FAMILY ARK Noah had his ark—here's your chance to build your own. It's easy: Just start naming animals and work your way through the alphabet, from antelope to zebra.

WHAT I SEE, FROM A TO Z In this game, kids look for objects in alphabetical order—first something whose name begins with "A", next an item whose name begins with "B", and so on. If you're in the car, have children do their spotting through their own window. Whoever gets to Z first wins. Or have each child play to beat his own time. Try this one as you make your way through zoos and museums, too.

JUMP-START A CONVERSATION

WHAT IF...? Riding in the car and waiting in a restaurant are great times to get to know your youngsters better. Begin with imaginative questions to prime the pump.

- If you were the tallest man on earth, what would your life be like? The shortest?
- If you had a magic carpet, where would you go? Why? What would you do there?
- If your parents gave you three wishes, what would they be?
- If you were elected president, what changes would you make?
- What animal would you like to be and what would your life be like?
- What's a friend? Who are your best friends? What do you like to do together?
- Describe a day in your life 10 years from now.

DRUTHERS How do your kids really feel about things? Just ask. "Would you rather eat worms or hamburgers? Hamburgers or candy?" Choose serious and silly topics—and have fun!

FAKER, FAKER Reveal three facts about yourself. The catch: One of the facts is a fake. Have your kids ferret out the fiction. Take turns being the faker. Fakers who stump everyone win.

KEEP A STRAIGHT FACE

"HA!" Work your way around the car. First person says "Ha." Second person says "Ha, ha." Third person says "Ha" three times. And so on. Just try to keep a straight face. Or substitute "Here, kitty, kitty, kitty!"

WIGGLE & GIGGLE Give your kids a chance to stick out their tongues at you. Start by making a face, then have the next person imitate you and add a gesture of his own—snapping fingers, winking, clapping, sneezing, or the like. The next person mimics the first two and adds a third gesture, and so on.

JUNIOR OPERA During a designated period of time, have your kids sing everything they want to say.

IGPAY ATINLAY Proclaim the next 30 minutes Pig Latin time, and everybody has to talk in this fun code. To speak it, move the first consonant of every word to the end of the word and add "ay." "Pig" becomes "igpay," and "Latin" becomes "atinlay." To words that being with a vowel, just add "ay" as a suffix.

MORE GOOD TIMES

BUILD A STORY "Once upon a time there lived..." Finish the sentence and ask the rest of your family, one at a time, to add another sentence or two. Bring a tape recorder along to record the narrative—and you can enjoy your creation again and again.

NOT THE GOOFY GAME Have one child name a category. (Some ideas: first names, last names, animals, countries, friends, feelings, foods, hot or cold things, clothing.) Then take turns naming things that fall into that category. You're out if you name something that doesn't belong in the category—or if you can't think of another item to name. When only one person remains, start again. Choose categories depending on where you're going or where you've been—historic topics if you've seen a historic sight, animal topics before or after the zoo, upside-down things if you've been to the circus, and so on. Make the game harder by choosing category items in A-B-C order.

COLOR OF THE DAY Choose a color at the beginning of your outing and have your kids be on the lookout for things that are that color, calling out what they've seen when they spot it. If you want to keep score, keep a running list or use a pen to mark points on your kids' hands for every item they spot.

CLICK If Cam Jansen, the heroine of a popular series of early-reader books, says "Click" as she looks at something, she can remember every detail of what she sees, like a camera (that's how she got her nickname). Say "Click!" Then give each one of your kids a full minute to study a page of a magazine. After everyone has had a turn, go around the car naming items from the page. Players who can't name an item or who make a mistake are out.

THE QUIET GAME Need a good giggle—or a moment of calm to figure out your route? The driver sets a time limit and everybody must be silent. The last person to make a sound wins.

THEMATIC INDEX

PARKS AND GARDENS

PERFORMANCES

PLANES, TRAINS AND AUTOMOBILES

RAINY DAYS

ACKNOWLEDGMENTS

Several folks were essential in putting this manuscript together. I thank, first and foremost, my husband Jon Cross and daughter Zoe, who were willing to go anywhere and do anything in the name of research, and my son Remy, who didn't give me too many problems with morning sickness while I was writing. Thank you to my editor at Fodor's, William Travis, for his careful eye and diligent work. I'm also grateful to Stacy Shugerman, friend, photographer, and impromptu babysitter, for her unflagging assistance. Finally, I'd like to acknowledge the county of Miami-Dade for providing so many wonderful indoor and outdoor playgrounds, where children of all ethnicity can play together rain or shine, speaking the language called Fun.

–Jen Karetnick

the end